Youngest Son
OF A MILLIONAIRE

By
Paul Ventura

This book my only justice for the Ventura family

ISBN: 0615664849
ISBN 13: 9780615664842

Library of Congress Control Number: 2012912130
CreateSpace, North Charleston, SC

DEDICATION

For my father, who made me the man I am today.
And for my children, who make me, every day,
want to be a better and better man for their sake.

PREFACE

Frequently America is depicted as sort of a great ladder. On this ladder, many remain on those lower rungs, struggling to move upward and onward. Others sputter and stop after some initial success, held back from the top either by circumstance or character. Many believe and hope that, in the United States more than in any other country, that ladder lends itself to any stubborn or persistent individual's climb. Those who still believe in the American Dream insist that whoever wants to reach the top can strive and achieve his or her goals. Americans are dreamers, pioneers, risk-takers. The country's success is built upon people with fantasies of making it to the proverbial top. In those dreams, once the struggles have provided a way up, there is no coming back down. In the American Dream, there is not supposed to be the greed, manipulation, or corruption that push families off the ladder. Thus, the dream is delusive. In the end, those tangible, material items that evidence your success no longer remain. All you have left are pictures and sentimental items, which have no dollar value but to look at or hold just brings you pain or sadness.

As the youngest son of a millionaire, I have climbed up that ladder and back down again. I stood high upon the top step, the ladder my father built, with my family by my side.

But as much as this book centers on my father, Joseph Ventura, this is my story. Of course, the two of us are inescapably intertwined. Still, my story is based on proven facts, documented court cases, stacks of paperwork, phone conversations with lawyers and bankers and government agencies and three court trials. In my story, the protagonist faces tribulations, enjoys successes, but makes mistakes. He also copes as his family falls apart amid accusations. As with so many family tales, there are episodes of backstabbing and, in our case, that age-old problem was perhaps made worse by the alcohol abuse that loomed over my mother. Dad's death brought on all sorts of suitors, drawn like moths to the flame of his real-estate empire. New scoundrels vied for the role of family patriarch, sowing seeds of discontent among siblings and squandering whatever they could get their greedy hands on.

Facts are facts. Anyone who questions the validity of my claims can verify my story with the bankers and lawyers who betrayed our family's trust. On this journey through the story of my life, you will visit the District Attorney's Office, the Governor's Office, the Attorney General's Office, the Board of Bar of Overseers and, as a last effort, the FBI. I wrote letter after letter to various government agencies throughout the Commonwealth of Massachusetts, but my efforts were met by a brick wall and deemed unwarranted. All too frequently, I didn't even receive the slightest hint of interest regarding an investigation. Nor did they offer to take a second look at my case. Though I have the evidence to prove many criminal and unethical business transactions took place, rarely have those with power troubled themselves to investigate—a sad fact that has taken a toll on my faith in my home state of Massachusetts. These documents tell of deceitful actions, all too often in the paradoxical form of inaction, which left my family with no chance of saving what was left of a multimillion-dollar estate that my father built this empire with his own hands makes the pain all the worse. But what stings the most is the betrayal of the people my father trusted to care for us after his death, those who destroyed our family with greed, manipulation, and dishonesty. My hope is that this book will serve the cause of justice and free me from my frustration and anger toward those involved. For many years I have not been able to let go of these events. What I share with you henceforth comes from the bottom of my heart and is true; however, it is time for me to present these memories and facts within the broader context of history. In the name of my father's hard work and commitment, I can only hope that my dad, Joseph Vito Ventura, is looking down on me and giving me the strength to tell this story accurately and well.

It is a complicated narrative as it involves many turns and a number of colorful characters. The games were fast and furious even before he was buried, and the players—both insiders and outsiders—included my father's trusted bankers and lawyer and friends. While nothing will ever repair the damage, I write without bias knowing karma and the world will give right back to them what they have doled out to us. In the interim, I pray for them, "for they know not what they do."

This book isn't all about corruption. Though my life has been plagued by its share of pain and disappointment, a major part of this story is about my family's happy times together while my father built his empire. Dad was unlike anyone I have ever known. He was beloved by all those who knew him. As harshly therapeutic as it has been, my writing is the only way to guarantee my father's hard work, insurmountable generosity, and love for life and family live forever. This story is the product of years of research, pain from trying to win a losing battle, and my acknowledgement of a never ending battle Above all else, this is the tale of one of the most wealthy, well-known, small-town families that eventually disintegrated, with family members ultimately turning against each other: Ventura versus Ventura. Every experience—from absolute bliss to the depths of despair—along with all that my father taught me, both directly and by example, have made me the man I am today. I treat others the way he taught me. I own my obligations as he so often demanded. I am a full-time, single father to a young son named Mateo—a bundle of blond hair, big blue eyes, and a warm heart. Mateo, whom I live for, is part of the reason why I am writing this book. I want him to get a glimpse into my life and that of his grandfather so that he has a permanent image of that man's greatness. I also wrote this for my older son, Paul Joseph, named after both me and his grandfather, and my beautiful daughter, Nicole who in my eyes will always be daddy's little girl.. They did not know what was happening to their family because they were too young to understand it as it was happening. After reading this book, I hope they realize what I have done to hold the family together and honor my father's legacy.

* * *

It hurts to look at the photos of my family's former properties. Despite being told by Christ on the one hand and Lao-Tse on the other not to get wrapped up in the material temptations of this world—and to focus on spiritual rather than monetary wealth—I can only say that neither spiritual leader actually lost such a fortune due to other people's meanness and greed. The Buddha willingly gave us his kingdom and the benefits due to him as a prince, but it is an entirely different thing to have your kingdom stolen from under your feet as you grieve the man who built it.

My father went for an eclectic style when he chose a building to buy or to build. Since leaving his original appliance business in order to buy the land under his store, my father applied basic real estate principles ("location, location, location," as the saying goes) in buying various properties to enrich our family.

Dad saved money on all elements of his transactions. Before he bought, Dad was the master of due diligence. Afterward, he always worked on the buildings himself—and later delegated these tasks to my brother and me—to save on contractors. We rebuilt tools when they broke and always tried to do the right thing for the building, the community, and ourselves. We made sure that those who dwelled in our buildings could rely on us.

Our strategy centered on permanence: buy it, fix it, and rent it out. Even though I suggested it several times, my dad couldn't grasp the concept of flipping properties as you see nowadays on TV. We weren't the kind of fly-by-night operators who try to distract from the cracked foundation with new kitchen counters. We would fix the foundation. After all, we wanted to invest in the long term.

We rented to banks, the Social Security Administration, and the IRS. We built those banks, built that IRS building, and added on to the smaller Social Security building. We had offices and apartments in small cities just outside Boston, close enough to keep the commute reasonable but far enough away that small-service businesses and residents wouldn't break the bank paying for the necessary square footage.

This was no Rockefeller's or Carnegie's fortune, but it was a well-developed and sustainable business while we had it. My dad was the center of it all, though. And as soon as he was buried, his lifetime of work was buried, too, beneath false legal pretenses and shams. The story of that process is a long and demanding one to navigate, one with legal twists and turns, deceit and outright fraud, and family dynamics that would make a Shakespearean royal family blush. The short version of my family's downfall is that other people stole what Dad had worked so hard to build. The motivations and mechanizations behind that theft, as I've pulled at loose thread after loose thread, are by no means short or easy to understand.

If my dad had made more effort to act like the rich landowner and leader of his community, had taken on some of the trappings of his status and used those to his advantage, the firestorm following his death would probably have been less terrible and not as all-encompassing. Perhaps others viewed my family as simple-minded or somehow easy prey. They certainly viewed Dad with doubts because he refused to indulge them and play their games. I don't remember my dad doing much glad-handing or making nice with the other centers of power like the city council or any other business leaders. He was his own man, to the point that he had fewer allies in the power structure of the town.

But he paid no attention to any of that political nonsense and instead just kept working right up to the end. Why navigate social politics when you could go out and look at concrete property? Considering the health benefits of taking it slow and getting out for a nice walk, or of doing some cross-country skiing, I will always wonder if I shouldn't have encouraged him to play more rounds of golf with his peers. With all the news about the consequences of stress upon one's health, I know that Dad's workload didn't do his body any favors. With a bit more time off, would he have lived longer? Who knows? It is probably a moot point because the man was generally incapable of taking a load off and relaxing. Would engaging more in the political and social structures have given others pause before engaging in thievery? Perhaps.

Of course, the real reason these people did what they did was probably more due to something present (greed) than something absent (affection or connections). After all, Dad was worth around fifty million dollars at the time of his death. But those who pulled on that money were not just distant businesspeople in the broader community. Family too came a-calling, epitomizing Humphrey Bogart's sentiment, "Ten thousand cuts a lot of family ties."

DAD

Who was Joseph Vito Ventura? The words on his headstone *born March 12, 1932* and *died January 14, 1983* suggest a life cut short.

The Ventura family had six children: three boys and three girls. Only one of those children would go from poor Italian kid to multimillionaire. Dad was the youngest of three boys. My twin uncles and my three aunts were all wonderful people. My father had helped each of them at one time or another because that's what family does. Generosity was second nature; he went out of his way to help people when they needed it. He was also thankful for all the generosity he'd been shown and all the lessons he'd been taught when he was younger.

He told me that we weren't any better than anyone else. I vividly remember interactions in the bucket seat of his old Ford truck. We'd be driving to a site and would see someone in ragged clothing, perhaps pushing a grocery cart. Dad would notice them first, and it never failed that he'd stop the truck and point his finger.

"Look over there, Paul. You see those people?"

"Yeah."

"What would you call those people, Paul?"

"Homeless, I guess."

"That's what I thought you'd say: 'homeless people.' You know what I call them, son?"

"Nope."

"I call them 'people.' And they are every bit as human as we are. You better remember it, too. We could easily be in their shoes. If it hadn't been for the lessons I learned from my family, and the lessons we are trying to teach you, I could easily be homeless—or poor—just like them. We aren't any different. We've just had better chances. You hear me?"

"Yeah, Dad."

"And I have some news for you. The breaks we've gotten, Paul, we have to make the most of those breaks. Otherwise, the people who worked to give them to us worked in vain."

Dad was certain that our good fortune was a fragile thing based on a combination of hard work and luck. In that view, we easily could've had the modestly successful lives of our neighbors who lived and worked from paycheck to paycheck. And we could have had much less: no vacation spot on the lake, fewer toys on special occasions, and so on. Part of what infuriates me so much about the squandered kingdom Dad amassed is that he was so cautious, so careful, and so mindful of risks. And when he was gone, it dissipated as if it had never existed.

He was not always serious. He was particularly passionate about Boston teams, and I do remember the times he'd cut loose watching sports…at least when the Boston squads were winning. We went to quite a few Patriot's games when I was growing up—a couple a year. The guy who did our excavating work on the bigger construction sites had season tickets, and in a casual sort of quid pro quo he'd offer us a couple of games a year. Dad drank his beer and ate peanuts while I gravitated toward the more sugary treats. Rarely in our house did I get to enjoy the amount of sugar in that cone of cotton candy and giant Patriot's soda.

When we weren't at the games, and if the game was blacked out on the local television networks, my brother and father would drive up to the camp house in Hillsborough, New Hampshire, to watch sports. The recent success of Boston area teams was in those years a distant daydream, as they all—with the exception of the Celtics—pretty much stank. Nonetheless, Dad had made sure when he looked for a cabin site to find the edge of the blackout zone for Boston sports affiliates. I've often wondered why he didn't go to the bar to watch with other guys. It seemed that most of the construction workers who worked on site with us had stories to tell about the pubs the night before. But then, Dad was not much of a bar guy. He was kind of a loner, and he certainly didn't go out cavorting and partying like Mom would do later in her life. He preferred, if he were to stop working at all, to spend time with us kids somewhere quiet.

He might have chosen the site for the cabin as a respite from the stress of keeping Mom on the straight and narrow. She struggled so much to maintain a steady routine and to avoid dipping too deeply into alcohol. With all of us kids, and with that added responsibility, he must have longed for a release. Perhaps that seventy-five-minute drive was what helped renew his calm. He never did mind driving.

Even though Dad was quiet and avoided going out on the town, he did have a fun side. Watching him night ski with a cigar in his mouth and catching air was one of those great you-had-to-be-there moments. It was particularly funny because of his build. He was strong but not athletic. He was a short and stocky Italian. When I say *strong*, I mean every ounce of him was fierce. He often challenged guys at construction sites to feats of strength. His favorite was picking up a sledgehammer, which must have been about twenty-five pounds, with his pinky and thumb. They all had to raise that sledgehammer all the way over their head. "Anyone can match this," he'd say, "you get a week's pay." People never could, though it was hardly from lack of trying. Dad would sit back and laugh as they tried in vain, chuckling heartily if they happened to drop the sledgehammer on toes in their distracted effort. He probably maintained his strength through insisting on always playing a role in the dirty work. He never avoided getting on his back with a wrench. In fact, the more grimy the job, the more he relished it. Given his normal level of intensity, it was especially fun to watch this serious and stocky fellow attempt—and fail—ski jumps of various types while chomp-ing on a stogie. We'd go to Crotched Mountain to ski as a family, though these occasions were too rare. Even then, Dad was cautious about the side he portrayed. After all, you never knew when you might see a business partner, and he didn't want anyone to think he was flaunting his wealth. So when we went skiing, Dad wore his old army jacket. This multimillionaire, who very well could have paid for the ski lodge itself, went humbly up the mountain's lifts in blue jeans, immune to the economic stigma of his clothing.

Dad wasn't frugal just for appearance's sake. His choices in clothing had a practical element as well. He was more business savvy than anyone I've ever known. Early on, though, we children tended to regard this quality as quirky rather than redeeming. He was immune to our perceptions and protestations because while we kidded that he was cheap and worried too much about public appearances, he knew that *everything* that affected his business's bottom line was worth tracking closely. This quality led him to look hard for deals. He'd spend days gearing up for big liquidation sales in the nearby communities, and he always insisted on buying in bulk to save a percentage on each item. With the range and num-ber of properties he owned, those pennies added up. He'd take an inventory of what we needed at the current time and make a second list of things that we'd likely need in the near future. Then, he would return from those sales with tools, plumbing parts, elec-trical switches, fixtures, and anything else on sale for cheap that he might one day need. At times, we'd use those materials even though something else might have looked a bit better.

Even though he liked to save money, Dad was driven by another, less practical motive: he loved auctions. I'd go frequently with him on Saturdays to help load items. He was like a kid in a candy store when it came to finding deals.

"Can you believe the pricing on those sink kits, Paul? Those go for five times that in the hardware stores."

"Yeah, Dad. Great."

My enthusiasm was a great deal less than his. Usually, at the end of a long day, the teenager in me was eager to head out with friends.

"Dad, I really am sick of being here. I told my friends that I'd be home by seven to go out with them."

"Well, Paul, I'm going to get this shower stall coming up in the next lot, and then there is a boiler that we'll need for the camp."

He was quick to remind us of the benefits we reaped from his bargain hunting. When Dad bought that boiler for seven dollars and installed it at camp, he gave me ceaseless grief on winter trips about how I liked the heat.

"Do you like being warm? If we'd left, we'd never have gotten this warm. We could have gone to hang out with your friends, but that would seem a lot less appealing if you were sitting here in the cold, huh?"

His persistence at times drove us nuts. But, on other occasions, we scored lucky personal breaks from his need to find deals. Dad rarely looked for anything but construction supplies, but if he saw something he thought would make his kids happy, he'd splurge. At one auction, a supply of dirt bikes came up for bid. He took one look at my wide eyes, saw how they were glazed over with desire, and bid on them. He ended up with two, plenty for all the siblings to go out cruising when we took family outings up to the cabin. Even as we celebrated, though, he had a moment of regret. Someone had come up to him after the auction and asked him why he hadn't just purchased the whole lot.

"If you'd have bought all of them, I'd have paid double right afterward. I couldn't believe that they just went with your first offer!"

Dad listened to these words with chagrin. He was more frustrated over his lack of foresight than he was excited to give those bikes to his kids.

We kids didn't just reap the rewards from these purchases, though. We also suffered from them. Once, my brother Joe was in a truck with two friends driving to New York City to pick up a shipment of wallpaper. He was supposed to take it back to Lynn, where we stored lots of stuff in the basements of the original building Dad had bought. Well, Joe wasn't paying any attention to the road. He was singing some '80s song by a band with big hair, and he was probably daydreaming about some girl at school, when suddenly his buddy started shouting, "Stop! Stop the truck!"

"What are you talking about, Hayes I'm ready to get there and get home, man. I've got a hot date."

"Stop the truck, will yaw? Now! Hit the brakes!"

My brother finally did stop, about a hundred yards from an overpass.

"All right. I've stopped. Now can you tell me why the hell I did?"

Hayes didn't try to explain. He just said, in a voice still a bit shaky, "Get out and come take a look."

Joe begrudgingly got out of the truck and walked around to the passenger's side. Hayes showed Joe the words displayed on the side of their truck: MAX CLEARANCE–14 FEET. Then he pointed to a sign on the overpass in front of them: NO TRUCKS OVER 13.5 FEET.

Joe whistled softly to himself as this realization suddenly hit him. He would have taken off the top of the supply truck! Instead of that route, he had to back the truck up a mile to the previous exit.

We might have had some adventures with Dad's auction bounty, but there was one thing we knew for sure: we never ran short of the necessary supplies. In fact, at times the manager of the local hardware store would call Dad to buy some of our stuff. Or, when Dad went in to buy something, he would use that chance to make a deal, mentioning that he just so happened to have five hundred one-inch paintbrushes. Since we needed some copper wiring, might the hardware manager be interested in buying a couple hundred? Indeed he might—deal! A profit was turned before we ever put much of those auction items to use. In exchange, we could expect great deals at that particular store. Everything was always on sale for us.

Often we found items that Dad could salvage. On one occasion, we found a ton of perfectly good marble during the renovation of the Eastern Bank in Melrose. We gutted that structure to do a complete overhaul, and behind the walls we found marble. Dad didn't believe me at first, but when I chipped some off to show him, he made sure to be there to supervise the process of taking it out. He knew how much it was worth. The minute we discovered it, Dad knew what he wanted to do with it. He had it recut, shined, and later placed onto the counters in front of the bank tellers. Marble wasn't the only thing we found in that structure. The building had, at first, been a skating rink. Then it was a movie theater. Then it was a VFW. We found all sorts of old stuff—lots of musical instruments, drums, bugles, and more. But with the marble, Dad knew that he could make a buck or reuse.

Dad had idiosyncrasies other than a fascination with bulk purchases and salvage operations. He also fancied himself an inventor. His goals weren't hubristic. He had no ambition about great fame or wealth from a quick break. He just wanted to make things better and more efficient. He took my old motorized trucks and tried to make an electromagnetic motor. He experimented with taking out the pistons and made friends with the local machinist. That guy loved to see Dad come in, as he knew when he saw Mr. Ventura that he could expect a big order of oddities.

Often Dad's inventions were practical responses to practical problems. Once, he was frustrated with the fit on our ice skates. He'd come to watch some of our games in the peewee hockey league. One time he'd noticed how everyone's ankles continually rolled and bent in with the pressure of pushing off the ice. He brainstormed for a couple of weeks on how to fix this particular issue. His solution anticipated the coming of Nike's pump basketball sneakers. Dad sewed a blood pressure sleeve into the inside of the skates and then tied the pump mechanism ball to my brother's hockey pants under the knee. After we put on the skates, he'd pump up the sleeve. Lo and behold...it worked! The Ventura's ankles rolled a lot less frequently after that. And Dad had the satisfied look he always got after solving a particularly intractable problem.

Another of his inventions was later validated with success, though Dad never saw it or reaped any financial rewards. I was reminded of this invention—he had made only a couple of prototypes when I was young—that he worked on for quite a while when I saw a device that functioned like Dad's self-closing hinge. Essentially, most doors have a closing mechanism that attaches to the door. Often this is a hydraulic pump—like what you would find on a screen door. Dad tinkered and tinkered until he invented a hinge that served this same function. It was spring loaded, which would have meant a much cleaner look on doors. A couple of years after he died, when I was going through some old papers in the attic of the family house, I found the briefcase containing all the patents. I vaguely recalled Dad's talking about this patent process. As I've started to see more and more of these self-closing hinges, I wish we hadn't let that patent run out. I wish even more that Dad had seen his tinkering recognized by the almighty consumer.

But I always loved looking at his projects, and I frequently begged him to bring me along. The range of his job fascinated me. At one building, he'd tighten up a leaky sink. At another he'd confirm reported leaks in the roof and then arrange for a subcontractor to come over. In many of those home calls, his services were as much emotional as practical. Many of the callers were older ladies who wanted someone to chat with, and Dad always obliged with a kind word and an open and receptive ear.

Dad's hobbies in those earlier years gradually became my own. In the reconstruction of old buildings, and during construction on new ones, Dad developed an interest in antique bottles. Anything with unique glass or an odd shape found its way to the floorboard of his truck, where it would clank and roll around until he found time to clean it and put it on the appropriate shelf in the kitchen. Old medicine bottles, glass Windex bottles, old Listerine bottles—their brands stamped into the glass to shed light on their previous contents—all of these fascinated him. Castor oil, 1906, Listerine mouthwash bottle, really small and round, and made by the Listerine Lambert Pharmaceutical Company, as indicated on the bottom. An old, local milk company bottle, shaped the same but much smaller. These relics from the past piqued his interest in history and mystery.

I started out as the cleaning boy on sites. As buildings progress, scraps of lumber and pieces of trash multiply exponentially. Cleaning up on major construction sites is a full-time—and minimal-skill—job. Perfect for a young kid who just wants to be with his father! After a while, I earned more responsibility. Workers began to trust me to put their tools away, a big responsibility. But I was attracted to the climate of the sites as much as the work.

Construction sites are worlds of their own, and I wanted to speak the language and observe the customs. As I put away tools at the end of the day, I'd keep a close eye on the card games that sprung up. Guys drank beers, and I'd watch their mannerisms. They ribbed each other, and I took note of their expressions and tone. I practiced my own tone on my siblings, and they often responded with the same level of sarcasm as the guys on the site.

Mom

Edith Bradley was a divorced, single mother of one when Joseph Ventura first laid eyes on her. Born on July 27, 1934, she had—by the time she met my dad—honed dark, almost black eyes that seemed to look right into your soul, long legs, high cheekbones, a prominent jawline, and a lithe, slender figure. Edith was absolutely beautiful. She somehow even made her coffee-shop uniform look good. One day Joseph just happened to stop by the coffee shop in Everett, Massachusetts. After stealing a look at Edith, he became a daily customer, determined to get a date from this beautiful woman. Later, Joe would share this story with his children.

"From the first time I laid eyes on your mom," he told us, "I knew she was the one I wanted to spend the rest of my life with. I had no doubts, kids. No doubts at all."

But Edith largely ignored him, other than refilling his mug when his coffee ran low. Dad claims that he knew this was the good kind of ignoring—the kind of ignoring that begged for more attention. As Joe turned to leave the shop that first day, he noticed her full lips turn up into a slight smile when this stocky Italian man in the black fedora assured her, "I'll be back again soon."

It took quite a while for Mom to warm up to Dad. Her reluctance was due to old scars; she had been burned in a relationship before, and she'd had a child—my half brother, Bernie—from that marriage to look out for. She rarely addressed that previous relationship, though it was quite clear that Dad was doing much more supporting, emotionally and financially, of Bernie than his biological father. Mom later claimed that she had been charmed by Dad's generosity.

"He was a good tipper, and he spoke to me as if he cared what my replies would be. I knew he cared by the way he stood still and looked into my face as I said anything. I could be talking about the weather, and he acted like it mattered."

She often laughed when she told us that he had not impressed her with his build. He was larger than life, she said, but a bit less than physically imposing.

As their relationship solidified, Dad insisted that Mom and Bernie move out of Everett, a big city, to live with him in Wakefield a small town, just twenty minutes north of Boston. Dad always loved Wakefield and thought it was the perfect place to raise a family of his own, with Edith. There in that Boston suburb, Mom and Dad would create a happy home for the Ventura children.

I remember Mom as a caring and put-together type of woman in whom Dad brought out the best. While Dad may have been a bit of a workaholic when it came to working on a property, Mom was the glue that held the family together. She ensured our sanity, as it was she who insisted that we take family trips for leisure and fun. She was the embarrassing mom who made sure we tucked in our shirts and brought our lunches to school. We grew up in the '60s and '70s, so gender roles were clearly defined and played out in our family: Dad worked and Mom managed the household and social obligations. Our laundry was always clean, quite an achievement when there are eight folks in a household. We always arrived at sporting events on time, and our dentist's and doctor's appointments, much to our chagrin, were always timely. She once escorted me to my first-grade class to say something to my teacher,

Mrs. James, and as she left she insisted, despite my protestations, that I tuck in my shirt. None of the girls in the class ever let me live that down.

But glue in a household is emotional as well as practical, and our emotional bond was sealed around the table. Mom cooked the best food that kept us gathering together, things that made us eager to break bread together. When we children came home from school, permeating our house was the mouth-watering Italian smell of Tomato and Basil simmering on the stove. Ziti Lasagna Ravioli -you named it, she cooked it. Though she herself wasn't Italian, she learned quickly that the way to please her very Italian husband was in the kitchen and on the plate.

She had a sharp side to her as well. She was continually fascinated by facts. She often helped my sisters with their schoolwork. She tried to help me, but I spent so much time working with my father that I became the kid who just barely graduated. Even when it became clear that I was not going to be the academic, she still encouraged my talents. She did not ridicule me or ride me too harshly about the things with which I struggled.

Well, Mom probably sounds like a regular Harriet Nelson, and we may sound like the Cleavers. Only one problem: Mom was an alcoholic. Though I now know that you can never be healed as an alcoholic, she had months where everything was fine. At other times, things were anything *but* fine. Alcoholics have a tendency to be as picky about their poison as any other addict. Vodka is what did it for her. Unfortunately, the guy who married her after Dad's death used that addiction for his own ends.

Nonetheless, none of us had the turbulent formative years as the child of an alcoholic. Mom and Dad were really great together and made each other better. She kept him on an even keel, and he kept her drinking, more or less, under control. He was always so stressed out about—or at least focused on—work. She cracked jokes, rubbed his arm and smiled, and did other things to help him realize that sometimes he just needed to take a proverbial breath. For her, the emotional anchor from her marriage kept her from flying off the handle. Still, there were warning signs. Mom fell down the stairs a few years before Dad died. She broke her wrist; it was a compound fracture. The doctors at the ER told us that she was so loaded on booze that she hardly needed anything to treat the pain. In fact, they couldn't operate on her until the next morning because the orthopedic surgeons were worried that her high alcohol content would adversely affect the operation. Having a bone protruding from her skin and feeling pretty much fine about it was probably indicative of where she was headed. In any case, it was a state that became more and more typical for Mom following Dad's death.

The suddenness of Dad's death probably threw Mom further off track than she otherwise would have been. But I'm certain that when Dad died, the best part of Mom died with him. Gone was her emotional anchor that saw them attempting to quit smoking together? Gone were the brakes on her drinking that got her home in reasonable shape? Shortly after Dad's death, the liquor had completely taken over her life. Her doctors repeatedly told her to stop drinking immediately or she would die within two years, which is exactly what happened.

Believe it or not, I'm not angry with my mother for what happened. Sure, she was the agent of misfortune. But my investigation later confirmed that others had preyed upon her alcoholism to break what otherwise would have been structurally sound estate documents. It's hard not to feel sorry for her. Because she was sick, people manipulated her into alienating her family and, in large part, dying alone. The deep, soul-sick pain I feel when I think of her on her deathbed is enough reason to forgive my mother.

Dad knew what would happen if Mom tried to manage the properties, and so in his final will were instructions for her care. He also left her with a generous monthly allowance. But due to an amazing firestorm of greed, his will was never executed. Mom got the loot and lost it all to her third husband and the people pulling his strings. At first, she'd tried to look out for her children. In fact, she even drew up a prenuptial agreement with her third husband to protect the assets for her kids, only to find that husband taken her to that same lawyer's office six months before she died and changed it from the Ventura children to himself .How the lawyer even did this, I would consider these actions a crime. My mother was so ill. Perhaps the saddest part of that story is I bet that she was so drunk, she didn't even realize what she was doing to Dad's legacy—or to her own children. Greed must be the worst and the most contagious of the deadly sins.

SIBLINGS

The Ventura family, like many families of the time, grew large and fast. Eventually Edith and Joseph had eight children: five girls and two boys together, and Bernie from Edith's previous marriage. I often wondered if Bernie ever truly felt as if he were a Ventura. He had his own last name. But more important, it was not Joseph's blood that ran through Bernie's veins; it was that of a man his half brothers and half sisters would never know. Although Bernie resembled Edith, certain features—including his round face and larger frame—set him apart from us. This mysterious biological father, a man named Bradley who abandoned his young wife and baby, never merited a mention from Mom. Bernie never spoke of him either, and I wonder if Bernie compared the two father figures in his life, one biological and one practical.

Early on, Dad revealed himself as a family man through and through, one who was determined to build a better life for his beautiful new woman, her son, and the many children that followed. Joseph, while being a man's man, had the heart of a saint with plenty of love to give. He wanted a large and happy family with Edith and, for many years, his wishes were granted.

The first child born to this new and happy Ventura family was Marianne. A precious young child, Marianne eventually took her place as both the matriarch child and the leader of any rebellion that stirred the Ventura house. I was four years younger than Marianne and passionately my father's son. As such, I have vivid memories of my oldest sister creating conflicts of interest for me as a brother and son. The boys she dated were always on the wild and crazy side.

One night, when my father was home playing cards with some friends, he asked if I would stay home and watch my sister with her boyfriend. Although I was four years younger, here I was, charged with making sure she didn't try to run away. I spent that night watching out the den window, and when I saw the thing my father had feared—my sister running up the street with her boyfriend—I dutifully ran to tell Dad. That episode created long-term tension between the Ventura's and said renegade boyfriend. On this particular occasion, my brother and I physically went after this guy. We all ended up in the neighbor's backyard. My Dad got into an argument with my sister, and that transitioned into a physical altercation with the boy. He ended up on top of Dad, and I went over to grab the guy by his neck. I squeezed and choked him as hard as I could. He got off and tried to spin me off, but as I distracted him Dad knocked him clean out. That was the first time I had ever seen Dad in a fight. He left no question that he knew how to handle himself.

Next in the line of Ventura's was my brother, Joe. He had a reputation as the clown of the family, a role he earned through his constant teasing and joking, but also from his ability to avoid taking things too seriously when others returned the favor. At times, he could be a bit harsh with his siblings, though that treatment probably just toughened us up for what was to come. I remember vividly how much he would torment my little sister while playing basketball with her in the driveway. He would let her score, and let her score some more, until she was on the verge of beating her older brother in a game. Then, he would storm back to take the game. He staged all of it just to watch her go ballistic following his comeback.

Joe was a competent athlete, and he always had the upper hand on me while playing hockey or other rec-league sports—and in the scrums that develop between all brothers worth their salt. He was handy and determined. On one particular occasion, he was determined to go out on a date with his girlfriend. There was only one problem: a lack of quality wheels. The family vehicle that Joe was using, a Jeep Wagoner, was on the fritz. It cranked only after we gave it some serious attention. Of particular concern was the battery. We had to do a special trick every time we wanted to crank it, as jump-starting was a bit harder back in those days. Joe knew well the limitations of his mechanical ability with that truck, but he was so eager to go out with his girl and so impatient with my methodical technique that he insisted on jump-starting it himself. I sat in the truck as he attempted to hook up the jumper cables. I watched through the crack between the hood and the winsheild as he mixed up the wires. Before I could say anything to him about the danger he was currently courting…BOOM! The battery wires sparked, and a massive explosion shook the truck. As I climbed out of the Jeep, quite literally shell-shocked, I looked to make sure Joe was safe. He lay on the ground cursing but seemed unscathed. How he came out uninjured is beyond me. His pride was another matter altogether. Our antics earned a bit of retribution from our parents. At one point, my brother had skipped school for two solid weeks. Again I was conflicted about my brotherly duties versus those of a son. When my father asked me, "Where is your brother? Why isn't he going to school with you?" I chose brotherly loyalty: "He isn't feeling so good, Dad."

Dad wasn't buying it, though, and dragged him out of bed and sent him off to school. He always could read people like no one else I knew. He knew, on that occasion, that Joe was sneaking out and riding his dirt bike on the Wakefield roads with his friend. Dad knew, too, when he heard the story going around the neighborhood that someone had written FUCK on my neighbor's household ice skating rink, that my brother was probably responsible. Joe may have enjoyed a creative streak, but he could not avoid the piercing power of Dad's gaze. Dad could look right through you. On this occasion, like so many others, the neighbor did not take terrible offense, perhaps but Joe had to apologize to Mr. Furness, whose rink had been vandalized.

The next in the family line was my sister, Sue. She was perhaps the most talented of the siblings. She played the piano, banjo, and guitar, and she was creative with her drawings. Unfortunately, we don't see as much of those talents these days. She seems to have let go of some of those passions. She always helped me shuffle girl-friends on the phone. She'd cover up for me when I was out with one girl and one of the others called. She would even encourage others in the family to just let it ring.

"Don't get it unless you are ready to lie for Paul. It is going to be one of his girls, and they are going to want to know where he is."

She could also play the role of Judas in the family. Once, when I was trying to keep from my father my first tattoo, she saw it and came over to lift up my shirt. She knew exactly what it was, but, nonetheless, she asked loud enough to get Dad's attention, "What is that?"

Sure enough, Dad looked over. I think we both expected him to hit the roof, but he was actually pretty cool about it. He gave me a bit of grief, but I knew how to respond.

"Dad, you have one."

yeah, but mine says 'Love you Mom.' It's a tribute to my ma. Yours is a picture of a dragon. A bit different, don't you think?" (Dad never missed a beat.)

Then Sue would resume her role as protective sister. "Different strokes, Dad."

Later in life, once most of us had started working for the family business, Sue was great about making us lunches. She never complained about these offerings of love to her siblings, this routine that required her to feed us at lunchtime. She was always there when we came home, and she patiently took care of us. We thanked her too infrequently for that kindness.

Dad had a particularly soft spot for Sue. She played the piano for him and made a special effort to learn all his favorite songs.

He rarely even got onto her when she came home with a damaged automobile, an event that happened too many times for it to be written off as coincidence. Often cars would not start after nights of her use. But the biggest regret I have with Sue pertains to my own actions. She and my friend Ralph got married. I thought they'd be great together and that it would be nice for me to have a friend become part of the family. Little did I know that their relationship would end in divorce?

The next in this auspicious line of Ventura siblings was...me. From the outset it was clear that I didn't take to school. My first report card is a classic reflection of what my teachers thought of me. They marked the grade "fair" for reading, phonics, and arithmetic. But their comments on the bottom portion of the card are hilarious. Apparently, I'd had an attitude. "Paul can be a bit fresh," one teacher said. I also was "frequently inattentive" and had "failed] to complete [my] work." I don't know what this means for a first-grader, but apparently I was "somewhat immature" and did not "work well independently." What first-grader *doesn't* fit that particular bill? The things about my personality, though, and my ability to connect with people, are probably truer today than ever before. My teachers thought that I was a "very cheerful" kid who "enjoyed his classmates."

As I grew older, I developed an affinity for girls, trucks, and hard work. I might've been a little bit on the crazy side, but my heart was in the right place, and I always cared about the needs of others, especially the elderly and people who were going through hard times. I loved working beside my father, even though he often gave me the jobs that took extra drive. I took on his challenges with enthusiasm. Jackhammer the wall for the vault in the bank on a long night until early morning? You've got it! Lay brick for days on my hands and knees? Sure thing! Work twelve- to fourteen-hour days for seven days a week to meet a deadline? Well, Dad was right there with me, so if he could do it, who was I to complain? Dad did recognize on occasion that I had elements of my life to lead. He often insisted that I go see my girlfriends, or knock off a bit early to go meet up with friends. I will say, though, that he just as frequently refused my requests to do the same. Sometimes we could take the time off; sometimes the work just had to take precedence.

The proudest I ever saw my dad was following one weekend when I was in high school, when I fully implemented his prime value, "Have some sense!" One weekend, as Dad and Mom pulled into the camp in New Hampshire, they were greeted by the blue lights of a Police cruiser. Dad was speaking with the Police Officer, upon which he learned that I was the only one of my friends who had not broken into the camp to steal booze. In fact, I had refused to go along with those friends and had warned them that it was a stupid idea, that they should think about the consequences should they get caught. My father was so proud. I was smart enough not to go along with my friends' stupid idea on a drunken night out on the boats.

The younger sibling closest to me in age was Diana. She was dealt perhaps the most difficult hand of all the siblings, yet she may have played hers with the most grace and courage. When she was born, and diagnosed with muscular dystrophy, the doctors told my parents that Diana would never walk. Both of my parents refused to believe this. With his own money, as insurance was no help, Dad had my sister undergo many surgeries. After one in particular, in which doctors broke her bones for some reason still lost on me, she was in a body cast for close to a year. At night during that year, the siblings would wake up upon hearing her cry. I would then bang on her cast to try to relieve some of the itching that was driving her crazy. To this day, my sister walks, drives a car, and goes to work every day. She actually wrote a book, *Our Fractured Wholeness*, about her difficulties. It documents how she has overcome the various obstacles life has placed before her.

My sister, Edith Ann, also called Edy has always been the brains of the family. She always gave me advice on different things that she thought I should or should not be doing. I never took her advice, though at times I wished I had. She rarely took mine, and often she based her own decisions on a fearlessness that drove me nuts with worry. I remember telling her before she went up to New Hampshire not to get out on the ice with the snowmobiles. I got a call the next day that she and her friend had gone through the ice with a snowmobile and crawled for about a mile back to the camp on hands and knees. Edy was relieved that they were safe but not apologetic for refusing to listen to me. I was so mad at her stubborn mentality. She could have killed herself and her friend. The day Dad called me to come up to help pull this snowmobile out of the lake, my cousin Eddie overheard me.

"I have a scuba suit that is warm enough for me to go under," he said.

We used a come-along that we attached to a rod we drove into the ice to pull this machine up out of the lake in the middle of February. I think that may have been the most harebrained project in which I've been involved.

Edy wasn't just bold on the lake when it was frozen. One summer day out on the water, she and an exchange student nearly got themselves killed. He drove too fast and, she, in an effort to save my boat, dove to kick a Jet Ski away from a collision. I stressed to her when she apologized for messing up my boat that I'd much rather she emerge safe than the stupid boat.

The youngest of the siblings was Tina. She was a surprise to all of us, including my parents. We never thought my mother and father would have another kid, and yet here came Tina, the cutest and most lovable little girl you could ever hope to see. Because she was so young at the time of my father's death, she can never understand the magnitude of what she missed out on. Also, because she was so young, she probably suffered more abuse from the revolving door of crappy men my mom dated after Dad died. Mom's alcoholism also must surely have taken a toll and, to this day, my sister Tina struggles with alcoholism like her mother.

I've talked about all the kids except for one, my half brother Bernie. Perhaps I've held back because Bernie is difficult to explain. He spent a lot of time getting in trouble, getting arrested, and causing my father an enormous amount of embarrassment and frustration. I remember my dad buying Bernie a new car for graduation. Bernie promptly traded it for an old MG convertible. Dad and Bernie just had completely different perspectives on cars. Bernie wanted to look good, while Dad wanted something that would be efficient, affordable, and effective. The look on my father's face when he found out Bernie had traded the car was beyond words. At times, I wonder if Bernie wasn't much for brains, but I also have no way of knowing how he felt about his own father or his relationship with Dad.

At times his problems seeped into my own life, and not always in trivial ways. Once, as a young boy and aspiring fisherman, I dug for worms in what looked to me like an ample supply of potted dirt in the backyard behind the fence. I had no way of knowing that the dirt was home to Bernie's pot plants. While digging, I pulled out all the roots of his plants. I obviously didn't know what I had done, but Joe was old enough to know because he warned me of how upset Bernie would be when he got home. I knew enough by that time to act sorry when Bernie got home, and he took it pretty easy on me.

BUSINESS

It's no secret that the United States rewards entrepreneurial risk taking. This is the place where, if someone works hard and has practical smarts, he or she can get ahead, regardless of background or education. Dad was a savvy businessman who, like so many in America, turned something small into something bigger with elbow grease, ingenuity, and some luck. He started with a small appliance repair business out of his truck and house. Soon, he parlayed that into a building for that business. His mother—my grandmother—told him to take the title from her house to buy the building for the business. He did so. But as he started to think about the logistics of what room would be used for what, he realized that he had more room than he needed. So, he came up with a plan.

Dad decided to split the building into smaller segments. Sure, he'd get less per segment on rent, but he'd make more overall. The building had three business units and three apartments overhead when it was purchased. He split each of those apartments into two. As the money started streaming in following the partitions, Dad sold his washing machine business to his partner—his brother, John. Using the profit from that transaction, he started a building on West Wyoming Street in Melrose. That building would later have nine apartments.

By the time he was done, Dad's real estate empire spanned three big office buildings in Lynn 140 Union St and 170 Union St and the IRS building he built behind the larger buildings, two banks both dad built in Wakefield and Melrose, a twenty-eight-unit apartment complex in Melrose, Richardson Ave which was sixteen townhouses and the original West Wyoming structure had nine units. Under Cliff was the big, orange Victorian which had eighteen units, and it was my favorite building. Dad actually talked to me about what buildings I liked. Inside the Under Cliff building, I would go into the dumbwaiters, which went down into the basement and up beside the apartments. Historically, people had used them to bring up their groceries, laundry, and so on. I remember a lot of stained glass in the hallways. These windows were in the front and back foyers. Up above was a skylight. The light would beam through the top of the roof and shine through the colors, creating images on the walls. Some of the windows contained flower designs. In addition to the glasswork, there was an incredible attention to detail with the framework, the mantels around the fireplace, and the cabinetry. Some people had rented in that building their entire lives. After a couple of years managing those buildings, I developed relationships with many of the older residents. One of the things that made Dad the proudest of me was the rapport I developed with those older residents. Many of the older ladies, when Dad checked in on how I was treating them and working, told him that I was "the sweetest young man, like my own." Dad loved that I had those connections with the residents. Dad had a special place in his heart for the elderly. His mom, by the time he was a property owner, was not well. I think he felt some guilt about not being available to her readily and consistently, and he saw in these older people his own parents. Because he viewed them as his own, he wanted to treat them as such. For his son to do the same made his heart as both a father and son swell.

At these various properties, some obligations were constant and universal. For example, there was always landscaping work to do. We did plumbing and carpentry, tiling and so much more. We did that painting and roofing. And if nothing else, there were minor maintenance to be done.

We did not hire a property management group. For these structures, we were our own property management, which meant that when a toilet was clogged, or a faucet started dripping, or a big snowstorm came, we were the people responsible for doing the job. I have no idea how Dad managed it all before we boys came along to help, but he did.

Dad had such loyalty to all of those people who lived or worked in our structures. I remember one episode, in particular, when my father and I were out trying to keep parking lots plowed in the Blizzard of '78. During this storm, which took place on a Monday and Tuesday, thousands of people were stranded. Boston received a record twenty-seven inches of snow. One hundred people died across New England, and it was estimated that more than 3,500 cars were abandoned on the side of Interstate 95 as roads became impassable, snow piled up, and cars were buried. When Dad and I went out to plow, he sent my brother Joe with his friends in the Jeep Wagoner to plow as well. Since Joe had gotten his driver's license, he had enjoyed that new obligation and the small payment that went along with it. His friends rode along to help with shoveling. They stayed out a bit too late in the storm and got stuck at someone else's house after the roads became impassable.

Dad and I went in the old blue Ford to the community sand pile. I started shoveling sand into the back for some ballast weight, and a gust of wind arose suddenly. Before I knew it, my feet had left the side of the truck, and I was thrown twenty feet away. Dad was standing over me the next second. As he loomed over me, asking if I was OK, I laughed, a bit stunned by what had happened. I'd been blown into a fairly soft snowdrift, so I was fine. Dad didn't think it was funny. The magnitude of this storm started to dawn on him, and we went home to rest while we waited for it to break. When we woke up, the whole truck was covered in the driveway.

You couldn't even tell where it was, and we had to shovel for hours just to find the truck location in the driveway.

Despite the weather, Dad's sense of obligation piqued again the next morning. So, we made our way out onto the roads, plowing as we went, and headed toward the office buildings in Lynn. We plowed the parking lot of the IRS, and Dad went down to check the boiler room. As we continued plowing, and as Dad joked with me about burning up the clutch, we heard yelling. Two guys were calling us from the bank buildings. As I looked at their red eyes and ruffled suits, it dawned on me that they had been stranded inside the bank all night. I had no intention of shoveling these guys out. It was their responsibility, and I had more than enough to worry about. But I had no choice.

"Get out and shovel."

I protested against this unfair expectation. But Dad understood that those personal favors were in many ways the foundation of his business with the bank. Once we got the stranded businessmen out, we went back over and started plowing the IRS, Social Security, And Congressman's Office. All of those were part of our office complex two blocks away.

Some of these buildings Dad had built; others he purchased. He wanted the one on Under Cliff Terrace, the one with eighteen apartments, altered. He wanted to split the units in half and add a parking garage in the back. The units were huge. Remembering his initial success with splitting rooms, he thought that he could essentially double his profit if he created more numerous, smaller units. But his business plan drew the ire of the folks in Melrose who valued antiques. They wanted to make sure that the building's original integrity was maintained. Dad did, too, as that was one of the main drawing features of the structure. Taking away the old charm of the structure would have hurt his bottom line, and he was a bottom-line kind of guy. But anything he wanted to do to the building, the historical committee in Melrose pitched a fit over. Dad found out very quickly how regulations from all sides could frustrate a businessperson.

The work was often backbreaking and dangerous, but Dad relished it. In so doing, we earned some close friends. I think people respected my father because, even though he was eventually pretty rich, he never shied away from the dirty work. I remember one episode, in particular, that upset one of those workers. My dad had asked the backhoe operator if I could sit in the machine to keep me out of the way and from getting hurt. Well, as I sat inside the machine, I saw a dump truck backing downhill toward my father. I can see it still: Me sitting in a backhoe on the other side of the construction site frantically pulling on the arm of the operator, trying to get his attention. Then stressing out more and more about the fact that my father was about to be backed over by a dump truck. When I finally got the attention of the operator running the machine, it was too late. My father was under the truck. All I could see was his arms flailing, like he was swimming his way out from underneath the back end of the dump truck. My heart was in my throat. I didn't think I would see my father alive again. By the time I got the operator's attention, and by the time he'd reversed course to find Dad alive but raving mad at the lack of attention to detail, that operator was so upset that he refused to run the machine for the rest of the day and instead took me for some ice cream at Friendly's down the road. This is just one of the things I will never forget in the early days working with my father and learning something new every day. This was the first building in which I was involved—from what we called the dirt up. Four stories it rose. Four *proud* stories of steel framed in metal stud construction, with underground parking, balconies, and an elevator to boot. This was how Dad did business.

DAD'S DEATH

Dad's death happened quickly and without warning. One day he was his old ornery self, insisting that we work long hours to get a job done. The next he was hooked to an EKG machine and struggling with pain. Given his level of stamina and health in the days leading up to that hospital trip, we thought that even this would be just a blip on the radar screen. Surely Dad would be back to work soon. I wish now that we'd had more warning. I wish every day now that I'd known those moments in the hospital would be our last as father and son.

Dad had been worried for a while about a job for the bank. Bank leadership had started rehabbing an older structure next door to their main branch. The goal was to fix this structure and add offices, but they'd wanted to move slowly. Because almost all of the work was on the interior, it made sense to get the boilers up and running. The building needed to be heated so the contractors could work through the winter. Anyone familiar with the temperatures of a New England's January—or March for that matter, because old man winter sticks around through April sometimes—knows that winter temps are not conducive to any sort of work. So, the first thing the bank tried to do when they bought the building was start working toward getting the boilers working. They did what they so often did when an odd job needed done right—they called Dad.

I urged him to "sub it out," or find another contractor to take the task from his plate. I often encouraged him to find someone else, especially as I grew more and more worried about his stress level. He rarely took that advice, responding often with the cliché about wanting something done right and doing it himself. He also took those opportunities, when I urged him to cut back, to remind me of just how much I didn't know. "You don't know about the Depression" or "You don't know what it's like to go hungry" or—his personal favorite when I complained at all about overwork—"You can't imagine what it's like to wonder when you'll eat again. Go hungry for a while. Then you won't complain so much about getting off your ass and doing a good day's work."

As soon as I saw the boilers, I figured this task was going to be a big one. It was an antiquated system that ran on a different sort of oil. Most people in New England didn't even use heating oil; Natural Gas got us Yankees through the winter. Most of the boilers I'd worked on had type two oil, which is much thinner and, as such, more easily and quickly heated. Type four oil is found in bigger, commercial-type buildings such as factories or schools. I'd seen my share of bigger buildings and had still never worked on a set of boilers that used type four. Well, all of that changed.

At first we just tried to do some regular maintenance on the old boilers. And believe me, there was plenty to update and maintain. They were twin boilers, probably as big as a small motor home. We first changed tubes in the boiler at points we noticed leaks. From early on, the right one seemed to run better. The one on the left was a bit more temperamental. I grew to understand the mechanics of them under Dad's watchful eye. Essentially, the oil burns. Then, that flame is fanned by a big motor and fan. The resultant roaring flame heats up a big vat of water. The water then passes through tubes that create heat. The heat is pumped into the rooms, and everyone gets to spend their days sheltered from the cold!

We worked on those boilers for a couple of weeks, trying to get them up and running. They'd heat for a couple of hours, but then they tended to lose pressure. We'd replace a tube or tinker with the preheating mechanism for the oil, and then they'd work for a couple of days or more. But just as soon as we thought they were fixed, we'd get a call from the bank folks that they were back down. Luckily, no suits were working in the building yet, so all we had to deal with were the bank personnel sending in their security people to see if the heat was working in the building. Dad knew precisely what to say to them to ease the tension.

Finally, we gave up on the boilers. Dad recommended to the bank that they start from scratch, and, as usual, they took his advice. But now, how to get the boilers that would barely fit in an average garage out of a single, low-cut basement door? Once we decided to start anew, we started working on a way to cut out those boilers. We started with the guts of the beast, cutting along the outside of the tubes, which were as thick as half inch steel into sections. After cutting those with a blowtorch, we pulled the tubes out in larger sections. We'd pull them through the door with a chain attached to the truck, as they were simply too heavy for us to lift, and then load them into the back. From there, the scrap yard. After a couple of days, we'd finally hit a rhythm. It looked like we'd be done with this task in no more than a week, so I started to feel a bit better about things.

That Friday, I went to dump a load and came back to discover my dad's car was gone. There stood my brother Joe with the chain, getting ready to do another load.

"Where'd Dad go?"

"He went to the hospital."

"What?" I responded incredulously.

"Yeah…he said his chest was hurting."

"Wait, he said his chest was hurting, and you let him drive himself to the hospital?"

I was so pissed at my brother. How could he have been so callous? In my anger, I forgot to account for Dad's willpower.

"Paul," he said, "I offered. I even insisted. He wouldn't have it. He told me to stay here and finish the damn job."

"Well," I responded, grasping his perspective, "the scrap yard is closing in thirty minutes anyways. Let's just head to the hospital since it doesn't do us any good to load this stuff now. We'll get it tomorrow."

In the hospital, it was quite clear that Dad had too much on his mind. We had just completed a new bank in Melrose, during which we had worked a steady string of fourteen- to fifteen-hour days, and we were still fatigued from those months of effort. He'd only had a short time to catch his breath, and then the boiler project started. Plus, he was taking care of all the other properties. So, the fatigue from previous jobs lingered, and while Dad should have been worried about getting better, all he could think about were his finances and the looming responsibilities of his nonstop obligations. Now he was worried about his will. He wanted to see Mr. Goldman, the lawyer from the bank who had helped him prepare his will. No matter how many times he called, though, Mr. Goldman just didn't have the time to appear or even call back.

I believe the morning my dad died, Mr. Goldman had planned to show, but I was told later that dad had died only an hour before Mr. Goldman would arrive. Whether this is true, I am not sure. I am certain, however, that my dad had trusted Mr. Goldman.

The next day, Dad insisted we get back to work. So, we went back to the bank's new office building to keep ripping out those boilers. We'd had a fairly productive day, though only eight hours of it instead of Dad's preferred twelve hours, and headed over to the hospital after knocking off. When we got there, Dad was even more stressed. One of the reasons left me furious. It seemed that the bank president had called Dad—at the hospital—to complain about something that had not even happened! And who was actually responsible? My old friend, Randy. Calling him a *friend* is putting it nicely.

Randy was the bank's head of security. A big, husky guy with a beard that was going gray, he had a habit of sneaking up behind me when I was working on the boiler at the bank building. He wasn't just physically sneaky. He reported everything we did to bank leadership, and, in the process, he mostly reported lies. Whenever Dad sent me to do something by myself, this guy was always coming up behind me; it was eerie. You know how you just don't feel like you can trust some people? How they give you the creeps? Well, this was Randy. He was the bank's security guard, and it seemed as though the gun on his holster gave him a false sense of superiority. In any case, he was hell-bent on prying into our business. Apparently, he viewed us as incompetent and untrustworthy. I could not do anything to please this guy. One day, just as we were getting sick of dealing with those old boilers, I went to get them back up and running. I'd never done it by myself, but I had seen Dad do it countless times. I called him and told him that I'd found the problem: a tube was leaking a bit. I had a replacement part on site and asked Dad if he wanted me to go ahead and fix it.

"You sure you got this, Paul?"

"Well, you tell me, Dad. I just explained to you how I was going to do it."

"Yeah, you got it. Go ahead."

So, I cut out the problematic portion of the tube, installed the new one, and began the arduous process of getting the boilers started again. First, you have to start the preheat mechanism, which heats the really viscous oil enough so that it thins a bit. Then, the flames build up, and the water starts to heat as well. That day, I'd monitored all the pressure gauges just like I'd been taught. I made sure that everything was working well, even as Randy—yes, he'd made an appearance and didn't seem to want to leave—watched. After the boiler got up to pressure, and it seemed to be operable, I called it a job and left. The next day, Dad got a call from the bank president that the boiler had run dry and was melted and ruined. To hear that from the president was a bit odd, as he didn't know the first thing about boilers. But it was also false. I'd looked at the boiler as it went up to pressure. There were no leaks. Nonetheless, I knew who told the lie: Randy! Someone had tinkered with the thing. The float in the boiler, even if a leak had developed after I left, should have shut off the boiler once the water level dropped beyond safe levels.

The boiler nonsense was not an aberration. The day after Dad arrived at the hospital, Randy struck again. The bank president called him and told him that we almost cut a gas line during our day at work. Tell me, who calls a man in the hospital to complain about business? Regardless, the claim was that we almost ruptured—while winching out the remains of the old boiler—a gas line against the far wall.

Dad asked me about it as soon as I arrived at the hospital.

"Did you all almost bust that gas line at the bank office building?"

"What?"

My mind started spinning. Who in the world could have told him this blatant lie? I instantly thought of Randy. That pesky security guy had overheard me talking to the other guys working: "You guys be careful. We don't want to hit that line. If we did, we'd all go up in flames, and this basement would become your tombs." The guys had laughed at my dark joke, but apparently Randy took that and told the president that we almost blew up the place and burned it down.

I've run gas lines. I'd worked around gas. My main fault was probably around a topic as serious as gas. And perhaps the lines should have been cut off, from the outside of the building. But they were capped and sealed. We certainly didn't come anywhere close to blowing up the building.

Dad had far too much going on to heal and rest the way he should have. He was trying to manage his money. He kept frantically trying to get in touch with Mr. Goldman about his will. So, the bank had no trouble getting in touch with Dad about things they were frustrated over, but when Dad needed to talk about his finances, no one could be found. Goldman knew Dad was sick. Why didn't he respond? Too busy for my dad, I guess.

During those days, we waited anxiously for a diagnosis. Dad had severe chest pains that came and went, and the doctors at New England Memorial Hospital talked about shipping him to Boston. They were going to examine him for blockages in his heart by putting some form of dye through his veins. Then they would perform an MRI to locate possible blockages. But we never got that far.

When I visited Dad the day before he died, he was business as usual. "Looks like a Nor' Easter is coming," he said. "Do you have a schedule worked up to deal with the plowing? Are we all set if this storm dumps on us? Are the snow blowers ready?"

"Don't worry about that, Dad. I think we're set. I'm going to go make sure they are working first thing tomorrow morning."

He then looked down and noticed my boots. I'd just bought a new pair.

"Look at those new boots! Look at you all decked out. Where did you get them?

"Well, you are going to like this, Dad. I got them at Nick's."

"Nick's? Finally!"

Nick's was a cheaper shoe store. Dad had tried to get me to buy shoes there for years, but I had always resisted. I never found anything there I liked and had believed that the lower costs were appropriate for the lesser quality styles available. Nonetheless, as Nick's was right next to one of our apartment buildings, I'd stopped in there a couple of days before and seen some steel-toed boots I liked. Dad was so excited that I had gone. He was frugal to the last minute of his life, and one of the things that got him most excited, even on his deathbed, was saving money and getting a good deal. To see his son adopting that same value set made him truly happy.

The next morning, I decided to fix the snow blower before heading to the hospital. Dad had been worried a good bit about making sure we were prepped for the storm. When storms hit, after all, we had to take care of all the properties. If we wasted time on broken equipment, our tenants spent more time stranded in their homes, and thus spent more time frustrated with us. So, I was out back behind the building in Malden, working on the snow blower, when my mom's sister, Aunt Bettie, who lived in the house behind the building, came out her front door and almost ran into me.

"You need to get down to the hospital right now, Paul."

"Has something happened?"

"They wouldn't say, but you need to go."

So, I got into my work truck and drove from Malden to New England Memorial in Stoneham. As I exited the elevator, I could see the doctors and read the somber looks on their faces.

"He's gone," one of the nurses said to me.

As they said this, I was looking past them and down the hall. There was Mom crying as the nurses comforted her. Their visible sorrow unleashed a torrent of emotions in me. I knelt down, unable to hold myself up as my insides cracked into a million pieces.

* * *

McDonald's Funeral Home in Wakefield was a big funeral home. As our family sat in the front room of the building, friends and acquaintances had gone up to the podium to read and speak about my dad. I remember my dad's closest friends going up to his casket. I watched them closely. Knowing his card buddies felt at least shades of the same loss I was feeling brought me some measure of comfort. They, too, were devastated.

I think some of my sisters spoke about our childhood. But most of that day remains a blur.

All the bank guys came to the funeral. Two of the guys from the bank came over to my brother Joe and said, "We are going to need to talk to you." When Joe reported this to me, I felt no hesitation in getting whatever it was they needed to share out in the open. So, I walked over and asked them what was going on. But they insisted on talking later.

Mom called us into the office on Albion Street a few days later and asked us to sign the probate papers. Now that Dad had gone, Mom took it upon herself to settle the issues with the business. It wasn't that I didn't trust her, but I did know that Dad hadn't wanted Mom involved in those kinds of business affairs. In short, I thought it seemed a bit fishy. My sister Sue later told me that Mom had gone into the office the night before my father's death and drew up a will leaving all assets to her. It was when he was confronted with this piece of paper from Mom that Dad started to have chest pains and died. He didn't want anything to be sold, and I think he knew that Mom would just as soon sell things off than keep the properties and corresponding responsibilities. Mom was supposed to get a healthy check, and Dad certainly didn't want to cut us out. After all, we had helped him build his empire. But I figured that Dad had some sort of specific plan about what would happen when he died. And I knew Dad and Mom's marriage well enough to know that his plan probably didn't involve her running things.

Mom's sisters and family members started whispering in her ear just days after Dad died. They were all over her, surely just wanting a piece of the pie. Greed is an awful thing, and it's even worse when it pervades a family. In retrospect I've questioned the way those family members responded so quickly. Who knows? Maybe they had connections with the bank. And who knows whether or not Mr. Goldman would earn a bit more money through his deal with Mom than his deal with Dad? What I know for sure is the money my family lost on that deal alone would, through the years, be in the double-figure millions.

A couple of weeks later—and this was when I started to really suspect that people had some serious ulterior motives—I ran into an old friend of my father's from the bank. His name was Dick Tamborini, and he had been a bank manager at the Wakefield branch. In the past, we often joked about the latest attractive teller at the windows. My brother and I got to know him by plowing and landscaping that bank that we built on Main Street in Wakefield. I believe he had been in some of the board meetings with Dad, so he had been close enough to talk business with us. When I saw him, he asked about what was happening with the estate.

"What's going on with your Mom these days, Paul?"

"What do you mean?"

"Well, I've seen her up at the bank a few times, and she said that your father had signed an agreement giving her control over the estate."

"Yeah," I replied. "I don't think that's going to work well for anyone."

"I know, Paul." Dick said. "Your father didn't want that to happen. Your family was supposed to get checks out of a trust. No one was supposed to control the estate except a trustee for the bank."

"How did you know all this, Dick?"

"He told me. And I am sure he talked to Mr. Goldman about it, too."

"Oh, really?"

"Yeah. I think they had drawn up papers with plans and everything."

Well, that truly got me going. I called the president of the bank. What I got in that conversation was the definition of a concrete wall. At first, he acted like he didn't hear me. So, I rephrased my question: "Did you know that Dad had a will drawn up?"

Silence.

"Hey, you still there?" I checked for a proverbial pulse.

"Yes."

"Well, did you know that Dad had drawn up a will with Goldman?"

"Says who?"

"Dick Tamborini. He told me that he'd talked to Mr. Goldman about it."

"That document wasn't valid, Paul."

"Why?"

"Because it was never signed."

I was not present that morning at the hospital when Dad had no one to turn to. I wished I had let the snow blowers go and had gone to the hospital instead. And Goldman should have had the decency to bring this document to our attention. Even if it wasn't signed, the right thing would have been to tell the family what had happened—that my dad had died before the trust was signed.

"I don't know what to tell you, Paul."

"Well, let me ask you something. If your father was dying, don't you think you would want to know what his intentions were for the estate when he still had his right mind? Wouldn't it matter to you that events after his death were consistent with his wishes?"

"Paul, I don't know."

"Why won't you just show me this document?"

Again the silence.

"I'm calling a lawyer," I said. I had painfully reached the conclusion that this route was going to be laced with dishonesty, misdirection, and downright stonewalling.

But I didn't call a lawyer right away. A couple of months later, I was up in the attic of the family house rummaging through some of Dad's papers. Some elements of the business still needed tying up, and the loose ends were going to plague me until I dealt with them, even if I wasn't personally going to get any of the payment for that work.

Going through one of Dad's old briefcases, I stumbled across a document that had to do with a trust for my dad's properties. The subject line read, "Trust and Will of Joseph Ventura." As I started to look more carefully through the document, I realized just what I had in my hands: Dad's will! And, boy, did it take a different course of action than the one currently employed by Mom and the bank.

The legal jargon was tough for me to understand, but, essentially, money from all the businesses was—according to Dad's plan—supposed to be put into a trust. My father had around seven different businesses. Some of the buildings' names he'd kept, while others he'd made up. Then I recalled all the checkbooks for all the different properties. An administrator was supposed to distribute the checks. Dad knew, after years of keeping Mom out of the liquor cabinet, that if she got her hands on the estate, everything that he had built would be squandered. We would still work in keeping up the properties, but the money from the rent would come out. Any profit would be distributed according to a formula my dad devised. There was a bill with the document as well. Dad had evidently paid for the document to be produced.

I mistakenly thought this would be the remedy for the problems we'd recently faced as a family and as a business. I presumed that with this document, we could finally fulfill the plans for the business as Dad had intended. So, I called Mr. Goldman at the office number that was listed on the letterhead. He'd prepared the documents himself. I wondered why he'd never mentioned this before.

"Hello, Mr. Goldman?"

"Yes."

"This is Paul Ventura."

"Hey, Paul. What can I do for you?"

"Look, I have a document here that I just stumbled upon. Some papers."

"What papers, Paul?"

"Well, it says in the subject line, 'Trust and Will of Joseph Ventura.' It says that he paid it in full, and it looks like he paid a certain substantial figure for these documents to be drafted. And underneath that, it says some specific things about a family trust, about who gets what after Dad dies, and so on. It's really very different than what Mom is doing with the estate right now."

When he didn't respond, I pressed on for some answers. "How come you never told us about this before?"

A few moments passed. Then he said, "That was never signed, Paul. And no judge would have allowed this will or trust."

"Well," I responded, "I have a hard time understanding that. I never knew my father to pay for something that was unfinished. He was a businessman. He didn't pay for services that weren't fully rendered."

"But it was never signed."

"Well, I want to see the trust you drew up for my dad."

"That isn't possible," he responded.

"I just want to know what he was thinking, Mr. Goldman."

"Hmm…that really…well, it's just not a good idea."

"I see how it is, Mr. Goldman."

I spent the next few weeks in a daze, unclear on whether I was imagining that the bank was covering something up. I did not want to assume anything about these people with whom Dad had been so close, the same people who had provided us with so much business. I began to talk myself down off the cliff of suspicion, but then I saw Dick Tamborini, the manager who had told me about Dad's will, in the oddest of places.

I was in the local grocery store, Shaw's, picking up some things for the kids. As I came to the end of the aisle, preparing to pay for my groceries, I did a double take. The guy in the green standing at the checkout counter was Dick. But instead of his standard suit, he turned to face me in a green polo shirt standard for the grocery employees.

"What the hell, Dick? What are you doing working here?"

He looked at me with a pained and somewhat strained expression and hesitated. After a moment he said, "I can't talk about it, Paul. You'd better go."

He was flustered; that was obvious. He could hardly speak to me or even look at me. And suddenly I had a terrible new awareness. *Holy shit*, I thought. *I got this guy fired from the bank. What in the world is going on here?*

This interaction bothered me for a couple of days. I felt guilty. It also confirmed my suspicion: something fishy *was* going on.

After Dad's Death

In 1983, the year that Dad died, the media covered one story with particular relish. A group of criminals had stolen close to fifty million dollars' worth of gold bars from a vault at the Heathrow Airport in London. These thieves had meant to steal around three million dollars' worth of cash, and, when they entered the vault, they were surprised to find such a huge collection of gold bullion. It is estimated that more than half of the people wearing gold jewelry in England are wearing gold that these criminals stole. Only two of them were ever convicted, and the rest made off with the bulk of the money. It was a story of intrigue, of surprise, and one ripe for the cinema of Hollywood. *I've heard of robbing banks, but they robbed the banks' bank.* Daring criminals making off with some financial institution's money! It was easy to fawn over them. Few regular citizens could empathize with the plight of the bank, though people had much less difficulty dreaming up numerous hypothetical uses for their stake of the criminals' fortune.

Other crimes of greed and theft are not so glamorous. And not all victims are as well insured as banks. For our family, the theft to come was personal. It might have been made for Hollywood, but the drama would have a more tragic than daring feel were it shown on the big screen.

It did not take long for Mom to lose any self-control that Dad had helped foster. Certainly she must have felt herself spiraling emotionally, and so she leaned on the best crutch she knew: Vodka. She started going more and more frequently to her favorite bar, the Lord Wakefield. From what I could tell, she also started going earlier and earlier in the day. We children could hardly blame her. She had lost this man whom she had leaned on for so long. She lost the father of her children. She and Dad had entertained a working relationship at some points in their marriage and had become less openly doting, but there was still a spark within Mom, and that guy who'd fanned it for so long was now gone forever.

It didn't take her long, especially with help from the Vodka, to start trying to fill all those holes in her heart. The first man to enter the picture—and this was no more than three months after Dad died—was a guy named Dick Fries. We never heard much about the origins of their relationship, but it was clear they'd met at the bar. That was the only possibility when it came to meeting Mom those days. She spent all of her time either sleeping or drinking. We kids knew where to find her when we needed her, but we also came to know that when we went to get her at the bar, we could expect a shell of the mother we loved.

From the beginning it was clear that Dick was not interested in the baggage of Mom's family—us. He alternated between being openly hostile and vaguely rude to my sisters, and he got off to a really awful start with my brother and me.

At the time, I was living at home with my fiancée. Mom had started construction on a new home out in Lynnfield. Dad had purchased land to build a new house when he was still around. She had plans to move out and sell the old home, plans I would later take issue with. Regardless, I was living at home when Mom brought into my life a new live-in boyfriend. The situation was perhaps ripe for conflict, and conflict grew fast and furious.

We Ventura kids started to pick up on Dick's faults at different points, though we were perhaps most upset by this quick turn to another guy after so many years of marriage. We knew that our father couldn't be replaced. We just wanted Mom to show that she knew this, too. One of my first interactions with Dick led me to believe that he was either oblivious or inconsiderate. From the get-go, he started parking his motorcycle in our garage. This frustrated and inconvenienced me because I kept tools in that garage and valued every square inch of it. I'd have said yes if I'd been asked, but for him to just start moving in was a symbolic slap in the face. He had invaded my space and insulted my dad's memory. So, that negative tone resonated with another of his actions a week or so later.

I had put sod down on the side yard of Mom and Dad's house, and I was tending to it carefully. Part of me had taken on this project as a way to preserve the memories I had of Dad. He always cared about how things looked and insisted that we did as well. Sod takes a great deal of patience and care early on, so I was watering daily. I had gotten it through a rather dry June intact, so imagine my frustration when I arrived home to find a single strip, about the width of a motorcycle tire, taken out of my big project. Dick had a maroon 1972 Harley-Davidson Sportster—a nice bike. Apparently, he'd driven it right through the sod while it was damp.

I was furious, so I confronted him about it. "What were you thinking, man, driving through the new grass I just planted?

"I don't see what the big deal is, Paul. I'm sorry it bothered you."

"Being sorry it bothered me isn't the same as being sorry. I worked hard to make the yard look good. I'm sorry that you don't care about that kind of stuff, but you can't just mess up things at this house."

"OK," he replied.

I walked away, though I was furious with his inability to sincerely apologize. I knew this wouldn't be the end of our problems.

Things came to a head when he started showing the same lack of respect toward my sister Tina. She said initially that she didn't like him, but a couple of weeks after he'd started dating Mom, Dick started making inappropriate comments about Tina's weight. This was the last thing my sister needed following the death of her father. I mulled over how aggressively to respond to this new problem. I found my answer soon thereafter.

I had just gotten home from work when a friend of mine, Dana, met me at the door. "What are you doing tonight? You want to go out?"

"Yeah, just give me a few minutes to shower. We'll go out."

As I stepped out of the shower, I overheard Dick say to my sister Tina, "Are you sure you want to eat that? You need to think about cutting back a bit. Go look at yourself. You are fat and overweight. And now you're eating that?"

Right afterward, he called out to me in a belligerent and drunken tone, "Paul, you parked the truck so I can't pull in. Can you move the damn thing?"

"Meet me outside," I told him.

What happened next, I am not proud of. But I grabbed him and swung him onto the ground.

Later, Dana told me that my face had gone blank as I walked into the house, pulled Dick outside, and body-slammed him onto the ground. I then started shouting, "Why don't you say something to me about *my* weight, Dick? You think I look fat? You think I need to lose a few pounds?"

"What are you talking about?"

"You! Talking to my sister with that disrespectful tone and voice!"

I guess I'd lost it because after Dana pulled me off him, Mom took Dick to the emergency room. He had a couple of broken ribs, but Mom came back later and told me that she'd covered for me. She'd told the hospital that Dick had fallen down the stairs into the basement. Covered for me? Hell! I wasn't ashamed of it or anything. I think she told the neighbors the same thing when they saw him bandaged up.

If I had known what would happen to Tina later on, I would have kicked his ass for being so hurtful. Shortly after he left, she started to lose weight rapidly—too rapidly. Eventually, after investigating her sneaky methods, it was determined that Tina had bulimia.

She was probably around ten or twelve at the time. She had always been a kid who had things under control, which, I've heard, is one of the tendencies for girls with eating disorders. But it seemed that home life was a continued negative factor for her because she made it crystal clear that she didn't want to live with Mom. When she asked me if she could move in with my wife and me for a while, I didn't want to tell her no. But my now ex-wife, Kim, was dealing with her first pregnancy, and she had a hard time coping with the mess that Tina would make in our bathrooms.

This added yet another dimension to Kim's stress early in our marriage. Our conversations were like a broken record. "Paul, I don't know how much longer I can clean up for this baby and your sister. I am going nuts here!"

"Have some sympathy," I'd respond, knowing full well that I needed to display an ample dose myself.

"I've had sympathy. But I'm just about out of it."

"Well, you are going to have to dig a bit deeper. She is my sister, and we are going to help her when she needs it."

Soon, Dick wasn't just inserting himself and his lousy opinion into our family home. He'd started to interfere with business. After Dad died, I completed some work that he and I had talked about For the Under Cliff Terrace property. The building had really extravagant angles, which made it look nice. But it also made the repairs a nightmare. The roofs were a bit curved, and so when they started leaking, it was a big operation to repair them. The roof girders had to be cut special in order to redo them, but Dad had talked about how it needed to be done before he died. The tenants had also started to ask when that particular project was going to get started. So, I recruited some help.

At Dad's wake, a friend of my dad's named Louie offered to help me with any projects. He was a skilled carpenter, and he owned an appliance store in Wakefield called LAR. It was three months' worth of work repairing all the porch roofs in the front and rear. We set up staging to facilitate the work. It was a real process. Well, a couple of weeks after I finished all this work, I saw Dick Fries walking the property with some real estate agents. I'd never seen him at any of the properties before.

"Dick, what are you doing here?" I asked.

The agents looked at me as if they had no idea who I was. They were also annoyed at my interruption.

"Well, Paul, we're talking about selling this place."

"We? Who the hell is *we*? Who in the world do you think you are to get involved in this? I've just done all this work on this place—my father's place—and you come talking about it as if it is yours to sell?"

As he backtracked a bit, the agents scattered rather quickly. When I talked to Mom about this, she did her best to dodge the conversation. I pursued it doggedly, and she avoided it just as stubbornly. I think that she was ashamed to admit she was looking to liquidate some of those assets as a result of Dick's prodding.

Either way, the wheels had started coming off this train. Soon thereafter, Mom bought herself, after some encouragement from this new boyfriend, a brand-new Chevrolet Blazer, which happened to be Dick's preference. He immediately referred to it as "my truck." But I vowed to avoid conflict with him for a while, even about something as overt and ridiculous as this. I succeeded for a couple of months, even after Dick talked Mom into buying a boat and renting a slip down At the Danvers Port Yacht Club. Despite all of this, I kept my cool.

Then my sister overheard something that forced my hand. Sue, who did all the office work for the business, overheard Mom and Dick talking about selling the business and buying a marina down in Florida. They had been spending a week or two every winter month down in Florida, and now they'd—or Dick, rather—considered making that a permanent residence.

Because Dick seemed to have some sort of strange power over Mom for a while, and because things had been snowballing anyway, we Ventura's put some stock in the possibility of this harebrained scheme. So, my brother and I decided to pay a visit to the boat in Danvers port. We knew that we'd find them there. If we weren't looking for trouble, we were at least looking for some outlet for our frustration.

When we arrived, Mom was absolutely trashed. It wasn't surprising, as this was her general MO these days; still, it struck a particular chord.

We walked up to the boat, and she took note as we approached. "Hey, boys," she said, as she struggled to stand.

"Look at you, Mom. You are drunk."

"So," Dick said, "what is it to you boys?"

"Well, we boys think that you are taking advantage of our mom. So, for starters, that pisses us off. You think we are dumb. But we are watching you. You think you are going to steal what we've worked for."

"I'm not taking advantage of your mom. But you should leave since you can't do anything to change the way we feel about each other anyways."

"Can't do anything?" I shouted.

My brother Joe pushed him, but his physicality paled in comparison to mine. I once again laced into Dick with fists, but this time I was pulled away early by Joe. We heard cops coming. Mom had called at the first sign of conflict, and so we headed back down the docks to the parking lot. As the police walked by us on the docks, we tried our hardest to look innocent and unassuming. When we reached the truck, Joe was so nervous his hands were shaking. He couldn't even fit the key in the lock. I helped him open the door, and we headed back to my house. Along the way we talked about what to do about this guy. I was inclined to keep pressing, whereas Joe was the type to let things ride a bit more. I told him that we couldn't sit by idly.

"Don't you see what he is doing to us, Joe?"

"I don't know, Paul. I just don't know. I think we ought to just let her do what she wants."

"What about what Dad wanted? What about what he wanted for us? For his kids? This isn't *her* legacy here. She isn't the only one with something at stake, man."

LAWSUIT AGAINST MOM

What happened next reminds me of a great Shakespearean tragedy. In *Hamlet,* the young prince of Denmark must watch as another man establishes an inappropriate relationship with his mother and, in so doing, tries to steal his kingdom. Whereas Hamlet was encouraged by literal or symbolic ghosts to retaliate, I had nothing but my conscious to haunt me. Mom's deteriorating health and mental welfare kept me up at night. This man, I was now certain, did not have her well-being in mind. Dick was interested in sucking her dry of all that my father had tirelessly worked for. I needed to do something big—and perhaps legal—to prevent this man from robbing us of our inheritance and stripping my father of his legacy. I started by calling lawyers in the area.

At the same time, Mom took it upon herself, with Dick's help of course, to cut me and my brothers out of the company. A couple of days afterward, they fired me, took away my keys, and tried to kick me out of the old family house she had just sold to me. After they fired Joe and me, no one was there to address the myriad of problems that occur with a series of properties the scope of our family's.

Mom was back and forth to Florida, and she left essentially no one in charge. Sue was still working in the office but didn't know who to call when the tenants called with a problem because previously she had always called me. So, eventually they called me directly:

"I have a clogged toilet."

"My garbage disposal isn't working."

"Paul, I've been calling the office, and…"

A few times I repaired items for the few tenants I felt really bad for. I regretted so much saying, "There is not much I can do. I don't even have keys anymore. I am sorry."

In 1987, in response to Mom's restraining order and the actions she took against Joe and me, I filed litigation. After all, I knew from Dick Tamborini that Dad wanted something very different to happen with the estate. Our probate agreement with Mom wasn't being even remotely honored, and we worried that she was drinking too much to make sound decisions. We also knew that there was a will in place that would have prevented this very thing from happening. I knew that Mom had taken a document to dad on his deathbed at a time when he was trying to access the one he had prepared with Attorney Goldman from the bank. I also think he did not think his wife and lawyer was not going to do what he expected at the time of his death. I do think at the moments before dad's death he felt something very bad was being planned with all his Millions of dollars' worth of real-estate. I also believe this contributed to my father's death. If he had talked to Attorney Goldman he would have felt more relaxed. Then mom did what she did bring some will to sign that she drew up herself this is what I believe caused his death. My poor father what he must have felt when he was dying knowing that the people he trusted were going to break his trust for their own gain. I hope my dad knows I never gave up and will never stop fighting for what he worked for and wanted for his family when he died. This fight I believe will be for the rest of my life.

Nevertheless, Lovins and Diller were recommended because they dealt with family probate disputes. They seemed nice enough on the phone, so my brother and I decided to stick with that choice. My brother and I filed a suit, but the girls didn't want to be involved. They thought our mother was running the estate well enough. Later, they would learn otherwise.

I quickly discovered something that would hold true with every new lawyer who came along: lawyers charge *tons* of money. My brother Joe initially paid twenty thousand dollars, which, with my payment of ten thousand, meant that we paid thirty thousand early on. Very quickly, that sum of money started to run thin. So, in place of additional payment, I offered to do some work around Nelson Lovins' house. He mentioned during one of our conversations that he had been struggling to find someone to extend the asphalt driveway next to his house, which had a significant decline. He couldn't turn around and, in order to avoid an eleven-point turn, he had to back out into the street, which made him nervous. The project was going to involve major dirt work. Nelson had some masonry contractors give him a quote, but they had told Nelson they couldn't do it for a reasonable fee. But when I came to take a look at it, I offered to take on the project. If I had given him a quote, it would have been around fifty thousand dollars. But I didn't. This was my first lesson. I should have been much more official and much less friendly with this man. How was I to know that soon he would come after the family house?

When I filed suit, Mom was furious. But eventually she cooled down. She was having trouble keeping up with the lawyer bills, so when I asked her if there was any way to fix this, she recommended that we settle. Her lawyers were a firm called Peabody and Brown and, I doubt they wanted her to settle, they wanted it things to happen slowly. They dragged out depositions and court hearings and wasted countless hours. After all, one isn't ever wasting time when one is paid by the hour, right? All I wanted was enough for my family to get a new start, and some symbolic sign of the role I'd played in the construction of this empire. Before we got an answer from the court about the trust in question (my dad's old one), I talked to Mom.

"Mom, let's stop giving the lawyers all of our money."

"What do you need?" she asked me. "What would be enough to make this happen?"

But before I could answer, she told me that, in exchange for our leaving the business and leaving her and Dick alone, she would give us each pieces of property. To Paul goes the family house and the property in Greenwood, and to Joe the building in Malden (she'd pay it off for him) and the land in Messenger Court in Melrose.

We were reluctant at first to take even this. After all, we'd heard the rumors that Dick Fries' son was going around Wakefield saying, "The Ventura brothers are out, and I'm in."

So, although we were angry at her proposition, our entire empire was already on the verge of being pissed away. We figured that the settlement was probably the best we were going to get before the entire estate was flushed down the toilet of Mom's relationships and drinking. Mom seemed set on the offer, and the original settlement she offered was going to give us each a portion of the business, so we were somewhat happy.

When she delivered the settlement agreement, it seemed fair to me. I wanted to sign it, but Joe insisted that we let Nelson get a look at it beforehand. There was only one problem: Nelson was suddenly unavailable. I couldn't get in touch with him. We delivered a copy of the settlement to his office and called daily to check in with him. If he told us it was fair, we'd have signed it immediately.

I think part of the problem occurred before that settlement was even offered. It was then that Nelson had placed before me a piece of paper that, had I signed it, would have resulted in his getting the family home for payment.

When I refused to sign that document, Nelson was suddenly a lot less friendly with Joe and me. And he was suddenly much less frequently free to talk about the case.

In the interim, as we waited, Mom started to get antsy. I don't know how much legal advice she'd had in drafting that settlement, or how much she'd had to fight off Dick in giving us the offer, but for some reason she felt pressured to get it done—and quickly. So, we called our lawyer and told him that we were in a hurry. But we never actually spoke to our lawyer, only to his secretary. This process went on for a couple of days. She kept calling me, saying, "Paul, what is happening here? We need to get this signed. What is taking so long?" I had a hard time explaining to her that we wanted our lawyer to approve this, a fact we later regretted. I even went to Nelson's office trying to get back the settlement paper I left their days and not hearing back from him but It was not on his desk when I went there. Finally, Mom broke and revoked the settlement offer verbally. Later, we found out that Nelson had been calling her lawyers trying to get them to sweeten the deal, unbeknownst to us.

Bad news arrived, as is so often the case with legal storms, through the lawyers. I received a call from Nelson to come to his office. When we arrived, he squirmed and hemmed and hawed.

"So, it turns out that the SJC has named your mom as executor."

"But that isn't what Dad wanted."

"Even though it didn't name anyone in that document, your mom is the default executor based on Massachusetts law."

"But Nelson, the purpose of that trust was to protect the kids, and Dad surely had in mind the many dangers that we would encounter if Mom had control. Surely he wanted Eddie Waystack to be the executor."

"I don't know what to tell you all."

"Don't know what to say? That is what we are paying you for— to know. I told you we should have talked with Mr. Waystack!"

"Well, the court wouldn't have recognized his juries'—"

"Stop!" I interrupted him. "I don't know much about legal jargon, and I certainly continue to be befuddled by the ethics and policies of the legal community, but I know that Dad trusted Waystack. And I know that Dad didn't trust Mom to be the executor of the family estate. He knew how much that stuff was going to be worth with the long-term leases."

Nelson didn't respond to me. He just sat there, shrugged his shoulders, and looked defeated. I wondered where in the hell this guy had learned to "practice" law. Or was I sold out it definitely felt this way. And what happen later even more makes me wonder about the actions of Nelson. Despite the ruling, we went to Mom to ask for her signature, appealing to her matriarchal instincts. With her was her new boyfriend, who had the nerve to say, "There is absolutely no way she is signing anything."

Once I started rooting around and looking into the legal misconduct, I found that Nelson's lack of efficiency had actually cost us the settlement. I contacted another lawyer about Nelson actions during my case he told me that the one big mistake is Attorney Nelson Lovins made was he should have asked the court for a stay on the ruling on the case during settlement agreement I had with my mother.

Turns out Nelson says he was "busy with some other stuff," right up until the moment that settlement was pulled. So, he prevented us from getting this deal. And all he had to do in the interim, to preserve it until he had time to look it over, was to file a stay with the Supreme Judicial Court. He didn't do the one, simple thing that would have kept these particular hopes alive. In an even later development, had we known that Mom's death would have given us legal claim to the original offer again, we would certainly have taken note of that. But Nelson offered very little in the way of productive and helpful advice. All he offered was bill after bill.

Nonetheless, we had another immediate legal concern. I still had a court date for the unlawful termination portion of the case. The court allowed me to bring a suit against my mother for firing me from my job in the family business. I think the fact that I was married and had two children might have been the reason the court let Nelson bring this part of the case forward. So I arrived at the court, eager to see justice done. We sat and waited for our case to come up on the docket. As we waited, in our coat and ties, a new lawyer that Nelson hired in his firm during the time we hired Nelson. Her name was Judy Metcalf and was not the one who was to come to court today.

"Where is Nelson?"

"He sent me. He didn't think that there was much chance of us winning this second portion, since we've already lost the first."

"What? That is completely different from what he told us."

"I'm sorry, Mr. Ventura."

"Geez, so he is just throwing in the towel? Should you even be here? You don't even have any knowledge with this case "what the hell going on here"?

At this point, my brother Joe walked up. I looked up at him. "Hey, Nelson's not coming."

"What? He promised us he was going to be here."

"I know. I'm calling him. Do you have any change?"

I dialed the number. I had it memorized by this point. It must have rung for about five minutes. Finally, his wife answered. When she did, I felt a brief moment of relief. *He must be on his way! That is why he didn't answer.*

"Mrs. Lovins, this is Paul Ventura."

Reluctantly, and softly, she said, "Hey, Paul."

"Where is Nelson?"

"Oh, I'll have to get him to call you back. He is in the shower."

"In the shower? What are you talking about? I am at court right now. He is supposed to be here."

She evidently didn't know what to say to this, so she said again that she'd have him call me back. Then the line went dead, thus beginning what was possibly the worst moment of my life up to that point.

I looked at the lawyer from Peabody and Brown as he watched me turn now to this young attorney sent by Nelson Lovins. He looked from me, to her, and then back to my somber and shocked face. And he laughed. How I resisted violence remains a mystery to me.

I was *sure* I had a case.

I was also quite sure that I hadn't received enough legal services to merit a $180,000 bill, a figure that reached me by mail from the office of Nelson Lovins. He'd blown the case, blown our shot at not just financial, but perhaps emotional peace. And here comes this bill? He hadn't even shown up for our big day in court! After all the dirt work we'd done. After all the crap we'd gone through doing odd projects for him!

When I refused to pay the $180,000, Mr. Lovins filed suit against us for "failure to render payment."

At the time, I was working for an oil company. When I received that suit in the mail, I was home on my lunch break. I didn't clean up before I went over to see him. I was black with oil residue from head to toe. His secretary asked me who I was.

"Who am I? I'm the one who was screwed over by Nelson's lack of professional ability and etiquette."

"I don't know what you are talking about."

"Well, Lovins does. And I'm going to see him."

"Sir, I have to ring him first."

"Like hell you do!"

What Lovins was trying to do was hard on two levels. First, he was trying to take the most significant asset that I still had in my name. But the action probably made me madder because, in so doing, he'd also be taking a little bit of Dad away from me. On a financial level, he knew what he was doing. This fact is the most important. In fact if I had had signed or let my brother sign the paper that Nelson put in front of us he said was to make sure he would get paid for his work performed would have giving him rights to my home for the consent of a dollar through his secretary's name. So for Nelson's poor legal work and failures he would have taken my house because I would not have been able to pay the remanding fees. And also if he had done his job I would have had no problem paying his bill and might have been able to save my family. I don't think he even knows the pain his actions cased me for so many years.

The weird thing about this whole business with Nelson Lovins was: I should have expected it. My wife's older sister, Lisa, was working at the time for the firm Peabody and Brown. This was the legal team that was representing Mom. Lisa knew that I had some deals with Nelson that involved working for him in lieu of paying money. She knew that I'd made repairs on his home, had done the dirt work for his driveway, and had helped him move office buildings. In short, she knew that I had been scrounging to pay these outrageous legal fees. She repeatedly warned, "Watch out for Nelson Lovins. He is going to try to take your house."

It seems, in retrospect, that Lisa knew something that I didn't. She knew that those services I'd provided, though valuable on their own terms, were difficult things to which one could assign a monetary value in a legal setting. She knew that, although Nelson Lovins had gotten his money's worth out of the deals, he was just like any other lawyer. His greed would stir him to seek more. But

I had ignored her warnings and had blown her off. And now he was coming after the house. One lawyer that I talked to told me to let it go into foreclosure. And therein lay my main issues with lawyers. Let the house in which I grew up go to the bank? Let the memories that we had there fall prey to this legal battle? Lawyers all too often look out for their own financial interest. Moreover, they presume that what is in their client's best interest is what puts the most money in that client's bank account, rather than thinking about the complicated moral and emotional implications that their client's "best interest" inevitably entails. In short, "best interest" is usually a complicated concept, one that involves more than monetary dimensions. And this lawyer failed to understand the emotional components at play for me. I wondered if they had a similar component buried deep within them. Was there something about which they could think emotionally, rather than in the more financial terms of money and hours?

SELLING THE TRUCK

Though I was living in the family house, and although nothing had been legally finalized, at the time, Mom still owned the home. Everything in the business was still in her name. Still, I had long ago resolved to do whatever it took to keep the house in our family's name, even if it currently wasn't in my financial best interest.

Folks from the Eastern Bank had started to call me about payments on the mortgage foreclosure. I had not been paying the mortgage, upon Nelson's advice. He'd told me not to pay the mortgage because the loan was in Mom's name, and to pay him instead. Well, now the bank was foreclosing this house that Mom cared nothing for keeping. So, if it were to be saved, and to be kept in the family, I'd have to scramble to find around $10,500. That number represented the amount of mortgage payments that were missed during the latter portion of the trial. In response, I went down to those same people whom we'd worked for during my childhood, the building we'd been working on when Dad died—the buildings with the boilers—and brought with me a wad of cash.

How did a guy like me, against whom the world had conspired, and who had been unemployed for months, come upon a huge stack of bills? Well, I knew I needed to make a certain monetary payment on the house to keep it. And I really only had one possession that was worth any serious money: my truck. This truck was so fine—without question it was the nicest automobile I'd ever had the privilege of driving.

Back when things were good, Mom and I had decided that it would be an appropriate vehicle for all the different type of work I was doing for the company. She had, before her suitors came around, made those kinds of decisions like a good boss does to better a business. I needed something to do my job? Go ahead; get it. I went to the dealership in Arlington and picked out a new Chevy truck. I used it for hauling around tools pertinent to property work, landscaping, plowing, and so much more.

This scene that found me walking into the bank with the proceeds from selling that truck symbolizes well the changes that the business had undergone. It was truly a depressing sign of how far Mom had fallen. This woman was now refusing to bend in a legal struggle for the family estate, and the cost of that refusal was not just placing the family home in jeopardy. So much waste of money and dads real estate.

I woke up and rolled over in bed. "I think I'm going to the auction today," I said to Kim.

"What are you talking about?"

"Pat told me that there was an auction up in Peabody off Route 1. I think I need to go sell this truck."

"Well," she asked, "how do you know how much it goes for?"

"Pat told me that I could raise my hand if I agreed with how much it went for."

I had no choice but to sell the truck if I wanted to save my house. So, I went down to the auction.

It was intense, and this made me anxious. As the auctioneer made his way through the various lots and got closer and closer to my truck, my heart rate quickened. When he opened up the bidding on the truck, I was more than nervous. Even though I had the power to veto any bid I considered too low, it didn't feel like an option to me at this point. After all, what would I do without this money? The family's home would be absorbed by the banking industry, and then sold to someone uninterested in the history and my emotional attachments. I felt less pressure about how much money the truck would bring than I did about my lack of options if it didn't bring enough money to pay the bank. To compound my anxiety, the auctioneer was flying through the lots. He paused very rarely, and once he started rolling on a particular item, it was hard to follow who was paying how much. That energy he brought to the proceedings that pacing and excitement was contagious. All but the most experienced auction buyers let emotion and the speed of the proceedings lead them to buy something they probably shouldn't have paid for.

But these buyers were either savvy or reluctant. The auctioneer started the bidding at $2,500, a number I considered a bit insulting. By the time he was ready to call the winner, the number was just at $6,000. That wasn't even close to what I owed the bank, which was nearer to $11,000. But more than that, it wasn't remotely near what the truck was worth. I refused to raise my hand, which meant that I had refused the bid.

After that initial failure, I waited a couple of hours before the truck came back through again. I had to be at the bank by eleven O'clock and I knew that if I didn't have the money by then, I'd lose the house. My mind raced through a slew of terrible options if this last-ditch effort to summon some money failed. Desperation at my financial straits, once a powerful but vague feeling, started to take a more prevalent hold on my psyche. At that very moment, I noticed a guy in a nice suit. For some far-fetched reason, my heart leaped just a bit. This was the guy who could solve my problems. I had a feeling. He was dressed nicely, and the way he carried himself made it clear that he did not struggle with money. If anyone at this auction was meant to be my financial savior, this was surely the guy. I watched his facial expression as the bidding on my truck started at $5,000.

"We'll start the bidding at five. Give me five thousand, five for this Chevy truck in great condition."

Hands started springing up around the auction floor. The nicely dressed gentleman was one of the bidders, but there were others who continued to drive up the price. As hands rose, so did my hopes. The numbers went higher and higher in thousand-dollar increments, and then, as the pace slowed, in five hundreds. Once it went past ten thousand dollars, the shades of hope I'd felt early on turned to full-fledged relief.

By the end of that bidding process, the price had reached $12,500. I worried that it would never get that high again, especially if this guy in the suit wasn't there for the third time that the vehicle came up for auction. So, I raised my hand when the auctioneer looked to me for approval. I even gave him a thumbs-up.

Once the bidding had stopped, and the excitement had faded a bit, my thoughts grew a bit more introspective. It pained me to sign the papers because I knew that in selling this truck, I was also mortgaging my ability to make a living and to get around. It stood as a sign of family to me. I'd repaired Dad's buildings in this truck, plowed snow, did landscaping—you name it, this truck did it.

My frustration with the entire affair turned to vindication as I headed—hastily—toward the bank. I made my way into the particular banker's office that had been handling the mortgage business on the house. As I walked through his office door, I thought of the boiler directly underneath my feet pumping heat into this building. I knew this building like the back of my hand, and I couldn't help but cringe at the irony that this structure—which was supposed to be the source of financial stability for my family and me—was now one of many competing agents in our misfortune.

"Good afternoon," I said to the banker, with more than a twinge of aggression in my voice. He was less than eager to see me, as we had gone head-to-head frequently over the previous weeks.

I'd been planning the conversation as I drove to the bank, and I started with the same litany of pleas and complaints that I'd been offering this guy for weeks.

"Look, can't you give me a bit more time? What if you just rolled those missing payments into the mortgage? You are asking me for a huge sum of money here, and if you'd just put that into the mortgage, I could easily start with monthly payments."

"Sorry, Mr. Ventura," he said, not a bit sorry. "My hands are tied. Those payments have been negligent for months, and our

66

policy states that the only way owners can redeem that negligence is with whole deposits. You'll owe us the full fee of ten thousand dollars, as I've told you, or your house will go into foreclosure."

"But it's the family home. The same family that built two branches for this bank. The same family that slaved away in the basement on the boilers. We worked for you, and this is the way you work for me? Don't you have any sense of compassion?"

"It isn't about compassion, Paul. It's about business."

By this point, I'd explained to the bank how the mortgage payments had grown negligent in the first place. It wasn't that I didn't have money to make the monthly payments. It was that Nelson Lovins, in his infinite corruptive spirit, had persuaded me to pay him instead of on the home. He'd told me that, since the home was still in Mom's name, I'd do better to pay him than on something I didn't yet have clear ownership of. I'd complied, reluctantly. And now, after Nelson's screwing us over, I looked to lose the house, too, if the bank had its way.

But, I knew something that this guy didn't. And, as he stood to usher me out of his office, I stopped him short. Can I ask you a question?

One last question.

"What is that?"

"Do you take cash?"

"Of course we take cash. But isn't that your problem? You don't have any."

When I reached inside my shirt and pulled out twelve thousand dollars in hundred-dollar bills, you should have seen this guy's face.

He stammered and stuttered, and then his face turned red with anger. He realized that I'd just played him. I think my dad might have been with me that day I really believe that to be true.

We didn't really acknowledge the negatives of the last year or so, but around this time Mom stopped spending quite as much time in Florida. I think Mom had a couple of brothers—our uncles— who died, and we attended the funerals. There, everything was cordial. We hugged Mom and offered our condolences. In addition, even during the settlement disputes, I'd take my children over to see Mom on her birthday. We always had big family dinners to honor birthdays, and it was important to Mom, as mad as she was at me, to have her grandkids at those parties. It also became clear that Dick had been the instigator in many of those choices Mom was making because without him around, things began to get better. Our access to Mom continued to improve, and then it took a rather dramatic swing when word spread that Dick had died quite suddenly. We didn't see Mom for a while, but when she returned from Florida, no one said much about where she'd been. We were just glad to have her back. And we were glad to find that the family business was opening up to us again. We wanted to do what Dad had taught us, in the places Dad had taught us to do them. It seemed that things were starting to look up, a source of great personal relief, and also a source of relief for the marital stresses that my wife and I had been feeling. Unfortunately, those suitors who were after our estate were not finished. The worst was yet to come.

LORNE

In the Greek story of Odysseus, when the hero left town, suitors came out of the woodwork to please his wife, Penelope. They tried every which way to win her favor. They knew that if they could, they'd have access to the significant fortune that Odysseus had left behind when he departed on his great journey. And in our modern American home, it felt that there was no shortage of aspiring romantics. But in our story, Mom was no Penelope. Odysseus's wife, Penelope, came up with numerous clever ways to delay, ignore, and frustrate those suitors. She remained a model of marital fidelity, and she was rewarded for remaining loyal to her beloved with the greatest of gifts: when her true love returned home, she had waited for him and preserved the opportunity for reunion. Mom, on the other hand, didn't seem too interested in preserving any remnant of the history she and Dad shared. She just went from one suitor to the next. The next suitor, after Dick, was Lorne. Our family would not survive him.

Much of my mom's life during this period was a bit hazy to me. She had moved out of the family home, and I saw her a bit less frequently than I had in years past. So, this guy who entered her life next made fewer appearances than Dick had, and for months he was just a name. Mom went down to the bars every evening, like clockwork, and her place of choice, as I mentioned before, was the Lord Wakefield. She'd head there every night around half past four.

A couple of months after Dick left our lives, my sisters started reporting that Mom was talking more and more about this British guy she'd been running into at the Lord Wakefield. It was appropriate that they'd met over booze, as that would later be the staple of their relationship. His name was Lorne Buchanan. It was an odd pairing from the start. She was fifty-six when they met, and he was thirty-eight. You do the math. It makes you wonder just how frequently relationships in which the two parties are eighteen years apart in age are based on genuine emotion. I'm guessing the percentage is low.

Lorne had done some construction before he met Mom, and I had heard of one of the companies with whom he'd worked Carlson Company out of South Boston. But the first time I met him, and on those all-too-frequent occasions on which we saw each other, I couldn't help but be bothered by his perpetual smirk. He was not a tall or imposing guy in any way. He stood around five foot eight and had a sort of wiry build. He also had a look that would drive any son crazy: the look of a fox or coyote on the prowl. Later he talked about the connection between construction and property management. He talked about how he could help Mom with all the obligations. But in all that talk, he didn't acknowledge that his knowledge of the former was a bit sketchy. And the things that happened after he fully exerted himself in the management side were certainly not pretty.

As Lorne became a more permanent fixture, it became clear that he had romantic aspirations for Mom that included access to her family business. He started going from property to property with her, looking things over and acting as if he knew what he was doing. But he didn't. He knew little about real estate and did not know the first thing about fixing things. For someone who claimed to have been involved in commercial fit-outs and renovations, as well as some minor carpentry work, Lorne didn't seem to me to know much of anything. He certainly didn't seem to understand the value of a dollar.

The incident with Lorne that sealed my understanding of his financial and practical ignorance perhaps also sealed our fate as enemies. I had gone to the property on 976 Main Street in Melrose to take a look at some of the laundry units in the basement. Someone had called in a complaint that one of the machines was leaking. Dad had passed that portion of the business to me. He told me that if I took care of the machines, then I could keep the profit from it. And who do I see there but Lorne. By that point, we had grown acquainted with his snooping presence, but this was different. I knew when I saw him that his role in our family affairs was growing like a cancer.

At some point around April of 1990, Mom married this creep. Their wedding was a fly-by-night type of thing. He'd been married before, and some of his family was there, but I don't think any of the Ventura children was even invited. In Lorne's previous marriage, he'd lived in California and had been behind on child support. He took money from my family—at the same time I couldn't pay *my* child support—and paid his support in full for the previous three years.

My friend Dana was living in an apartment upstairs in that building. He called me and told me that they'd started throwing away my tools. First of all, I had a beef to pick with Dana. They threw away my tools, and it took him a couple of days to let me know about it? What kind of friend was this? So, after that call, I hustled over to the building. Sure enough, the dumpster was full of my stuff. The underground parking at the building had storage closets that faced each spot. So, residents could pay for a spot to park and they'd get a bit of extra storage in the process. When we were done building the bank, we had no place to put all of the tools that we'd accumulated. So, I'd built a little shed on two of the car spots and with two of the closets. To throw away the tools in there was both stupid and insensitive. For one, the tools were really valuable. I really wonder were these tools ended up. Did Lorne get money for these or did he really throw them away. Even someone who didn't know what the hell to do with them could have sold them at a pawnshop for thousands of dollars. I had a bulldozer that I'd been working to restore, a transit for grading dirt, jackhammers—you name it, we had it. Tons of really expensive and industrial tools. I felt as if the world was turned against me. But what this person had done went beyond stupid and entered the realm of mean. How could I make a living without this stuff? Why someone would chuck that stuff is beyond me. But the broader question was: what in the world gave Lorne the right to throw away these things that belonged to our father?

I took as many of them as I could out of the dumpster and put them in my truck. I vowed to get the rest of the things the next morning. So, I awoke early and headed over. My heart sunk even further than it had the previous day. The dumpster was gone. Not just empty. *Gone.* I was devastated.

I was incredulous and confronted Lorne the next time I saw him. "What were you thinking? Why would you do that to me?" I shouted.

"Out with the old, in with the new, Paul."

"What the hell does that mean, Lorne?"

"We are goanna sell this building, and we have to get everything cleaned out in preparation."

"Says who?"

"Me and your mom."

"Well, you could have told me. Given me warning."

At this point, I realized that I had accurately registered his intelligence when it came to matters of property management. But I'd also dramatically underestimated this guy's ego and the size of his ambitions with our property.

Just a few years after their marriage, the Ventura Construction Company became the L Buchanan Company. His methods were mainly liquid. He made sure that, in order to maximize his influence over my mom, he kept her good and sauced. One of my sister's friends described an interaction she had witnessed one evening at the Lord Wakefield. Mom and Lorne came in a bit later than normal, and it was clear from the get-go that Mom had no business being in public. She could barely stand up. What does the responsible and respectable friend do? Get them home. But Lorne? He ambled up to the bar, a bit tipsy himself but certainly the person pulling the strings, and said, "She'll take a Vodka."

As the bartender poured the drink, Lorne looked back at my mom. She stumbled again, and he chuckled a bit to himself. He resumed his focus on the drink preparation and said, "Add a bit more Vodka, please"

Lorne started paying himself out of the family business, though for what I am not completely sure. He began to exert more and more control over the properties, and soon things started being sold.

I reached a breaking point financially at the same point that their spending caught up with them. Broken and worried about my own marriage, I went to find Mom to plead for some help. I was out of money. There was no money for food, no money for paying bills, no money to buy gas, nothing. I was practically starving. So, I took my son with me to see Mom. I felt as if that would pull on Mom's heartstrings some. Though she was never in the office anymore and wouldn't answer my calls if she saw my number appear on caller ID, I knew where to find her. I approached her in the Lord Wakefield, saddened to see her in the condition she was in. Even on a night when her drinking might help my cause by making her more emotionally open, I hated to see Mom like that. So, I started in on her and pled my case.

"Mom, I hate to come to you like this. But I can't feed my kids. I can't pay my bills. I don't understand why you are doing this to us."

"Paul, you have caused me so much grief."

"You grief?" I responded. "What about us? How are we supposed to feel? What are we supposed to do with the knowledge that Dad would be absolutely disgusted at the way you are living your life?"

On and on she listened. And it seemed as if she'd started to waver. I could see the sympathy welling up in her eyes, could tell that she was emotional. I've always worn my heart on my sleeve, a quality I got from her. But it seemed as if she didn't have the guts to make a decision, or couldn't make up her mind, so she turned back to the bar and muttered, "Ask him," pointing at Lorne.

First of all, I had some severe problems with asking this traitorous guy for a job in the company my dad had built and in which I had worked from my childhood. He was currently doing work that rightfully should have gone to me. Hamlet, when he went crazy in that famous Shakespearean play, struggled to cope with a whole ton of things. First of all, his mother took a new husband far too quickly. But, even worse than that, the husband then stole the throne from its rightful heir, Hamlet. It wasn't Denmark or anything, and I was anything but a Prince, but this empire was my birthright. It belonged to my siblings and me, and it would have been a source of pride and sustenance, until Lorne, like Jacob and Esau, like so many greedy people of this world, stole it. Despite my reservations about asking him, I sucked it up and said, "Lorne. What do you say?"

He sat with his back to me. "Lorne?" I said again. I figured he'd been listening to us, but he never even turned around. I knew what his answer was. The drive home was not pretty I could hardly see the road with all the tears I remembered looking in the rear view and seeing my infant son and knew I was screwed because I had no means to care for him.

DRUGS

Well, my mom and I were alienated from each other, and I couldn't repair the relationship, for a jackass was in the way. I could barely afford to feed myself; much less take care of my wife and kids. Although when I sold my truck I felt a tiny victory in going to the bank with enough money to maintain ownership of the house, I started to feel as if I had very little to live for. I had been struggling for months just to make ends meet, and now the primary means by which I had been earning an income—my truck—was gone. I picked up lots of odd jobs during this period. One guy in particular for whom I did a lot of work was Pat Drinkwater. He was introduced to me by a friend, and he essentially became a primary source of food and drink for a time.

Pat owned an automotive repair place in Wakefield on Lowell Street called Performance Plus, but he was also involved in a variety of economic enterprises. His automotive business did very well. In fact, he at one time worked on the black Mustang GT from the show *Spenser: For Hire*. Pat's income was not limited to his business, though. His house was one of the old homes that you see in New

England, and he rented out a couple of rooms in the back of that home. As such, he always had projects with which he needed an extra hand. I did some minor plumbing projects, some carpentry outside, and the installation and remodeling of two new bathrooms. All in all, at a time when I could find little work, Pat paid me well for these projects.

But our relationship eventually evolved into something a bit different, an evolution that was good for no one. For most of my adult life, like most guys who lived in the Boston suburbs, I attended the usual weekend parties and get-togethers. While there, I would usually drink a few beers. On a relatively rare occasion, those few beers would grow more numerous. Though I drank on those occasions, I never did any real hard drugs.

My drug use started with the occasional snorting. Pat invited me into his house one evening as I was finishing some plumbing work outside, and he asked me if I ever "liked to party." One look at the white lines set up on the table, and I fully understood his euphemism. I was reluctant, as always, but I'd just gotten another document in the mail from the Law Office of Nelson Lovins. I had been having trouble paying my bills and just that day had walked somewhere because I couldn't pay for gas. In short, I was in desperate need of an escape. So, I hesitated for a few seconds, and then I made a decision I'd regret for years to come.

My escape was snorting cocaine. This I did for just a couple of months, and then I transitioned to smoking. I still remember that first night I tried it. Pat asked if I wanted to take things up a notch, to feel "really high." My first puff on that pipe took me farther from my troubles than I had been in years. Instantly all I thought of was the next hit. Far away were those feelings of anxiety about income, and about the loss of a family legacy. The feeling was exponentially more intense. I was floating in a cloud, and all I cared about at that moment was preserving that cloud.

My hard core addiction lasted close to a year. During that year, my physical appearance grew unkempt and dirty. I became more and more skinny, and I actually ran out of holes in my old belt. Every now and then, during little snippets of sobriety, I'd look at myself in the mirror. There was no color, and there seemed to be no spirit or soul as well. My sunken face looked haggard. I knew that I would not last much longer with this routine. I was struggling to get work even more as I looked so ratty when I spoke with people about possible projects. That struggle added to a growing lack of motivation. *Who cares if I work? Who cares if I can pay the bills? Just keep those hits coming and I'm happy.*

When I was working for Pat, he more or less gave the drugs to me. He began to pay me in drugs rather than in money. I still don't know what he got out of that deal, other than someone with whom he could get messed up. But I know now, and began to know more and more then, that for someone who was struggling to pay his bills, giving up income for crack was not even remotely a good idea.

Nonetheless, this became more and more of a routine for me. I'd go over to Pat's house, smoke some with him and a guy named Lance, and waste the rest of my evening. I avoided smoking, even during the worst of this, during the daytime, but often I was up all night doing drugs, which made me pretty worthless during business hours.

Lance was probably—though I don't know this for sure—Pat's partner. Late in those evenings, they'd go into the bedroom after we did some drugs. They'd emerge an hour or so later, and we'd do some more. Meanwhile, I'd sit on the couch and watch TV. People around town knew the reputation of Lance and Pat, and I think they began to assume that I had joined in those sexual proclivities as well. I have always supported the right of gays to be with whomever they want to be with, but I was not with Pat and Lance as moral support. I certainly was not there because I'd grown any less attracted to women. I was there for the drugs. I was there for the escape. When I smoked, I got to forget about all the crazy shit going on in my life, and I relished that release. I needed, at those moments, all the escape I could get my hands on.

The only problem with using drugs as an escape valve is this: those things that I wanted so badly to escape weren't going anywhere. My issues with my ex-wife were only exacerbated during this turn to addiction. Nelson Lovins was still clawing for more money. Bills were still piling up at the house. And money was disappearing from my wallet faster than it ever had. Drugs seemed to have even more of an appetite for money than lawyers.

A couple of months into smoking, I expanded my territory of addiction. I stopped just doing drugs at Pat's, and in fact I started offering my house as a place to smoke. I had access to a better pad than most druggies, so I'd let folks come over to do drugs in exchange for a bit of a high myself. That particular turn led to a loss of my most valuable household possessions. After one evening of partying and smoking, I left a group of people at the house that I didn't know well. I had to get to work, and, even though I tried, I hadn't been able to rouse them. When I returned, sure enough, my TV, radio, and anything else they could pawn were gone.

The last night I ever touched Crack was a memorable one. When I arrived at Pat's house, he had a bigger stash than I'd ever seen him with before. I stayed around with him and Lance for a while. We smoked, listened to some music, and smoked some more. The issue I had started to face more and more frequently was that I had to do more drugs to achieve the same sense of freedom and release that I longed for. This is surely the predominant driver of overdoses. People long for that same feeling that initially hooked them, and, as they go searching for it, they find the grim reaper instead. Not me. For some reason, that night I took a look at the coffee table in front of me. I saw all the drugs I could possibly use this evening, and I knew without question that if I used as much as I wanted, then I wouldn't wake up the next morning. As soon as I had that thought, I did something that surely must have surprised Pat and Lance. I stood up and walked out, never to return. The walk must have been five miles. I was as high as a kite, so the lights looked weird to me as I stood at the crosswalks and tried to avoid jaywalking, and the consequent attention that would draw from police.

When I finally got home, it must have been three in the morning. Not surprisingly, all the lights were off in the house. No one was there, but the pictures on the wall reminded me of all that I'd lost. My ex-wife had taken most of the pictures that included her, but the kids looked at me from years past. I felt guilt at what I'd become. I vowed to change all of it, one step at a time. And then something happened that seemed to confirm everything I was feeling. One of those televangelists came onto the TV as I lay drowsily thinking of all the things I wanted to change. He asked questions that were worded broadly but that seemed to speak directly to my soul.

"Are you lost?" he asked, looking earnestly into the television cameras.

"Do you feel as if you can be more than you have become?"

With each question, I perked up a bit more.

"Do you feel a great void in your life? Are you facing issues that seem to have no easy answer? Have you reached the end of a particular road? Are you truly ready for a new beginning?"

As I thought, more and more vigorously, *yes* to each of these questions, I joined this guy in taking what he called the next step. I got down on my knees, and for the first time since my youth, I asked with great humility for help. I dedicated myself to God, vowing to do whatever it took to help myself.

RECOVERY

The next morning, the energy of that conversion was gone. The confused feeling I'd had when I got down on my knees had dissolved into something more vague. But the things I had taken from it were not. I was going to quit! The first week was the hardest. My resolve weakened toward the evening hours, and I'd find myself heading toward Pat's house. But just as surely as I needed that fix, I just as surely knew that I wanted no further part in it. Thinking of my father, of my children, and of the father I needed to be for them, I drew upon some strength I wasn't quite sure I had inside me.

Those around me who had accompanied me on my descent into addiction were not eager to see me go. People with whom I had done drugs sought me out, looking for someone with whom they could smoke. Previously, during some mild attempts to clean myself up and get off the drugs, when those guys would come knocking, it would strike a blow at my resolve, and I'd once again pick up the pipe. But after that particular night, after my walk and religious epiphany, when guys came to my house to look to smoke,

I'd lock the door. I think the difference was religion. I've always heard that AA—Alcoholics Anonymous—relies upon a faith-based approach. I'd never been an overly religious person, but I drew my strength from religion as well. I certainly didn't get a ton of help from the people around me. Only one person truly affirmed what I was doing from the get-go. Only one person bought the necessity of my imminent recovery as much as I did. He was a junkie himself, but he had tried to quit many times. He was, what I called, a reluctant druggie. One day, I ran into him at a bar. He asked if I was interested in going to another guy's house to smoke, and I urgently responded, "No, no, man. I am trying to get straight. In fact, I am clean."

"Huh," he responded, looking deeply into my eyes, ascertaining the strength of my conviction. He paused a second before speaking. "Well, if you are serious, here is some advice."

"OK," I responded. "Anything you got, man."

"Get a calendar," he said, "and put an X on each day that you are clean. That will give you some concrete symbol of your progress. Every day you add another X, say to yourself that you need just one more."

"One more?" I responded, a bit dubious about this lack of ambition.

"Paul, this fight is going to be day to day for you, especially for the first couple of months. And by the way, you aren't clean yet. If you can get a year of Xs, you are going to do it. And then, after you have a year's worth, only then can you look me in the face and say that you are clean."

This sounded pretty good to me. I liked the idea of something physical holding me accountable and reminding me of what I had done so far.

"If you miss just one day, Paul—just one—you not clean," he added. "In my experience, if you have been truly off it for a year, the cravings will be gone."

He was right. The physical cravings were the first to go. Then it was my emotional dependence. There were various levels of addiction, after all. The hardest thing to get past was the relief it offered from stress and pain. I just had to remind myself that those feelings returned in between highs, and when they did I had to face the fact that I had done very little about them during my drug-induced haze. Now, those drugs could be put right in front of me, and I wouldn't touch them. Not only that, I wouldn't feel tempted to do so. I had found other ways to fill and counteract those voids in my heart where my family, and all of its accomplishments, once resided.

Once I was a couple of months into my Xs, I got a knock on my door. I looked through the side window to see who it was. Armed with that knowledge, I was reluctant to open the door. It was Pat Drinkwater. I hadn't seen him in four or five weeks, and the last time we'd run into each other, he'd made a pretty powerful argument for me to come over to do a bit of partying.

"Hey, Pat," I said as I opened the door. "I hope you haven't come over here to recruit a smoking buddy. Those days are over for me."

"No," he responded. "That isn't all we were, Paul. We were friends, too. I came to offer you a name. I am proud of you for cleaning yourself up. There is this guy who can help you, I think. He has some work for you and will be a mentor of sorts as well."

I was more than a bit taken aback by this turn. Here was this guy who'd gotten me off the rails in the first place, now giving me a bit of a boost as I tried to claw my way back onto them. The gratitude I felt toward Pat is now tempered with guilt. I wish I'd done more to help him as well. A couple of years later, I found out that both Pat and Lance died of drug overdoses. Rarely does a day go by that I don't think about the fact that their deaths could very easily have been my own. But, things turned for me, largely due to Pat's help. The guy he introduced me to was a lifesaver. To this day, I don't know what he got out of the arrangement other than a bit of skilled labor.

The first time I met Bobby Brogner, Pat brought him by the house. He took a look at the physical mess, surmised that I was a similar mess emotionally, and started issuing ultimatums.

"Paul," he said, "it is nice to meet you. I am here to help you. But you have to agree to some things for me."

Who the hell does this guy think he is? was my initial reaction. But when I asked him to expand upon the sort of things he was talking about, the answer coincided with my own goals.

"You can't touch drugs. You have to totally give up the hard stuff. If I find out you have picked it back up, even once, we are done. You read me?"

"I read you," I told him. Then, I explained as proof the calendar with the Xs, which indicated, I assured him, that I was in agreement with him about the necessity of quitting.

"Who else is living here with you?" he asked. "I thought Pat said you were divorced and that your ex-wife had custody."

I looked into the den, where his eyes were resting on a couple of kids. "Oh, those are not my kids," I explained. "There is this guy living here—"

"Is he a renter?"

"Yes," I responded. "His name is Bob Weaver. He is my sister's boyfriend. I can't get his ass out of here, and I am so wary of cops right now that I don't want to get them involved."

Bobby responded, "Well, for now, while we clean you up, move in with me. I have lots of work I need done, and it will be easier for me to keep an eye on you with you close by. Later, I will deal with this squatter."

When I moved in with Bobby, there was indeed plenty of work to do. I retiled his bathrooms, remodeled his master bedroom, and remodeled the kitchen that went with his pool area. In exchange, he advised me on legal matters. When I got arrested, it was Bobby who went to the police station to bail me out. When the cops gave me the runaround on bail, Bobby was the one who went toe to toe with them. If I had a day in court, he'd lay out his son's nice clothes for me, insisting that I needed to look nice. He insisted that I fire my court-appointed attorney, a fact that made my probation officer more than a bit angry.

In those months, I found myself growing more and more clean. I thought less about drugs and more about what the future might hold. When I grew angry about the issues I was facing with my ex-wife, Bobby was the one who could talk me down and get me calm. I felt like I had finally found someone who was genuinely interested in helping his fellow man, and I was happy to be the recipient of some good old-fashioned grace.

Just as soon as I had moved in with Bobby, I moved out. This all took place under his direction and leadership. As I finished up a project on his fireplace, I remember vividly doing a bit of grout work on the multicolored tiles we'd used to cover the wooden mantel. I had blown off a wedding to finish this fireplace in time for a party that Bobby had coming up, and in exchange he had paid me a ton of money. He came into the room and praised the way the mantel had turned out. Then his tone changed.

"Paul, I have some good news. You are goanna get to go back home."

"Well, that sounds great, Bobby, but what about that jackass that has been staying there?" I responded. "You know he gets me worked up and angry."

"That is the best news of all, Paul," he said. "Bob Weaver is gone. I talked to him today. He'll be out by the end of the week."

I had no idea how Bobby had finally gotten through to this guy, but I was grateful. I think he had a bit more freedom to invoke the threat of the police, because he wasn't as shy about inviting them into a situation as I was. So, clean and sober, I moved home. I had reservations because Bobby had been such a safe and secure situation for me. But on the other hand, I was ready to start a new chapter.

Little did I know that this new chapter would involve a whole new round of problems. This time, the culprit would be someone I'd promised to love and protect, someone who had promised to honor me. Tell death do us apart.

WIFE AND KIDS

The difficulties that I was facing regarding employment and these squabbles with Mom took a toll on my marriage. My anger at Nelson Lovins, against my rational judgment and wishes, made its way into our house. I'll be the first to admit that during this period distractions adversely affected me as a husband. But, as the saying goes, it takes two to tango. If I walked us to the precipice, my wife helped push the marriage over the cliff.

As our financial strains continued to increase and I struggled to replicate the kind of living I'd been accustomed to working for the family business, my wife had started a new job. In my mind, this was a bad idea. I wanted Kim to be a mom, because I thought that, for her, focusing on this task would help her to be the best parent she could be. My mother had stayed at home for us, and I knew well the value of having someone there to support you when you inevitably needed it as a child. I also thought she might meet a new man at her job—and she did.

We'd had our good moments for sure. One of the things that kept us together was our common affection for the kids. She knew that I cared deeply for them, and I knew the same about her. When I met Kim, we were both still in high school. I must have been a Sophomore at the time and had gone over to work at my dad's building in Malden. While I was there, I chatted with my cousins Beth and Adele, who lived nearby. They were on the porch and were around my age. I hadn't seen them in a while, so we made small talk about the way that school was going and some parties that were coming up. But, I was more interested in the person standing to the side of them than I was in their chatter. I thought I'd heard Adele refer to their friend Kim before, but I didn't remember her saying anything about how beautiful this particular friend was. I played it cool, tried to feign a lack of interest, and vowed to ask the cousins about Kim at a later date. When I did, a couple of weeks later, they offered to fix us up.

Our first date was the typical teenage date experience. We kept my cousins Beth and Adele around as a sort of protective layer. The experience was less romantic than awkward. After all, when no one has a car, and when you are too young to go get into much mischief, what are your options for dating anyway? We walked around Malden Square. We went from store to store, acting interested in the merchandise but really trying to get a feel for each other. After our feet grew a bit tired, we ducked into a pizza place for some dinner. The girls talked, and I mostly just sat there. By the time we went to get ice cream, though, Kim and I had started to chat a bit more. When I walked her back to her house, I had a feeling by the end of the night that things had gone well. She seemed as interested in me—especially the construction stuff I was doing with Dad—as I was in her. After that evening, we dated on and off all through high school.

Toward my senior year, I grew particularly swamped working with Dad as we finished working on the bank in Melrose. He had made a promise to those suits at the bank about when the project would be finished. They had a ribbon-cutting ceremony planned for a particular date, and Dad felt obligated to finish on time. This would have been a reasonable expectation for all parties, except for the fact that this deadline had been agreed upon based on the plans for the building. But, when those suits at the bank made changes to the plans, they didn't make corresponding changes to their expectations of the time by which we had to be finished.

One particular example of this—and Dad probably should take the blame for this one—came with the construction of the vault. We actually built the vault at this bank, which was surely one of the most painstaking processes in which I have ever been involved. We got the plans from the architect, and though we'd never done any sort of concrete work even remotely like this vault, we figured it out eventually. We just weren't efficient by any means. The plans for the vault were that it would come up from the basement, and that the basement level would not be used for anything. Instead, it would just act as a sort of foundation for the vault room on the first, or ground, floor. Each of the walls on that basement level had three layers of steel woven into the concrete. The steel was immensely thick and heavy, and we had to lift it up, wire it in, and pour the concrete around it. After that, we had to do another wall just like it. Afterward, we'd move to another wall. And so the project proceeded, wall by wall.

At first, they were going to leave the basement layer closed off. But once he started to see the project develop, Dad talked to them about how much wasted space it was going to be. Finally, he convinced them and they changed their minds. Unfortunately, they changed their minds right after we'd completed the final wall. So, now we had to open up a door. We had to cut a hole through this wall we'd taken weeks to make impenetrable. The resultant change of plans took two days. I spent a fourteen-hour day working there. On the second day, I actually stayed all through the night with a jackhammer that continually grew jammed up in the layers of steel. Once I'd broken through the thick concrete in an area, I'd have to spend some time with a blowtorch cutting the steel. Delays like this cropped up throughout the bank project. And I learned early on that those delays, which were usually instituted by the clients, did not alter their expectations of the ribbon-cutting date. Thus, we found ourselves for the last couple of months working ridiculous hours. We'd wake up at seven in the morning and leave for the bank. We would not get back home until around midnight. We'd take a shower, dive into bed, and, before I knew it, Dad was in my doorway. I can still hear his voice: "Time to wake up, Paul."

The way he said it made it a nice wake-up call, as much as my body protested. When I struggled to get up, he'd grab me and pull me out of bed. What I still wonder is how Dad had the strength and stamina to wake up himself. A few months of that routine was hard even on my young adult body. I can't imagine how tired he must have felt, especially given the fact that his health must have been starting to fail him around that time. I say *must have been* because he never would have complained to anyone about his body.

During the last couple of months of work on the bank, we were mostly doing interior projects. We were hanging doors, starting to finish out the bathrooms, finishing the floors, installing carpet, and so on. And so I found myself in that bank in Melrose one evening with fatigue eating away at me. That feeling paled in comparison to my anxiety about this girl, Kim. See, I had developed a bit of a relationship with her, and then I'd sort of disappeared into work for months. Had someone asked me if we were dating three months ago, I'd have responded "absolutely!" But since I'd been away from her for so long, I wondered if that answer was still valid.

The worry began to grow on me more and more and I felt desperate about needing to see Kim. At the same time, I was torn by my loyalty to Dad and my pride. I wanted him to know that the work was as important to me as it was to him. But on this particular day, during this particular week, it just wasn't. I was smitten and wanted to do something about it. I finally worked up the nerve.

"Hey, Dad. I need to go. I haven't seen Kim in…" I tailed off as I tried to figure in my head how long it had been.

He looked at me knowingly and smiled. "Well, what the hell are you waiting for? Get out of here, Paul!"

But my delay in asking for permission to leave had cost me on the time front. It was late by the time I pulled up in front of Kim's house. I knocked cautiously at the door. Her mom came to answer my knock, already in her nightgown and dressed for bed.

"Paul? Is that you?"

"Yes, Mrs. Boudreau. I came to see Kim."

"Paul, it's too late, honey. You need to come back another time."

"I know it's late. But I got hung up at work. I really want to see her. I have been thinking about it all week, and I would really need just a few minutes to talk to her please.

I didn't even know if we were still dating. I hadn't seen her in so long, I was worried that she might have started dating someone else.

"OK. But you all stay out here on the porch. And she needs to come inside in fifteen minutes or so."

So, she got Kim, and we sat out and talked. I asked her if we were still dating, or if she had started seeing someone else.

"No, I'm not seeing someone else."

"Would you tell me if you were?"

"Yeah, I would tell you. Do I strike you as someone who is shy about the truth, Paul?"

After that moment, I wondered if we were going to stay together. Her reassurances were a bit tepid, and she didn't seem overly excited to see me. I took that as a sign that our relationship was breaking up, and we grew more off again than on again for a couple of months. For a time, I dated around and met another girl named Dolores. I liked her a lot, but she was slightly threatened by Kim. "If you go back out with Kim—" she'd say, and I'd respond, "Not happening, Dolores." We were at a time in our life when nothing about these relationships was really serious.

How could I know what was coming next? It was the biggest bombshell of my life. About three months after Kim and I stopped seeing each other, she called me and said that we needed to talk. I thought she wanted to get back together, and I told her that I thought we could do without any chatting, but she was insistent. She also wouldn't tell me what it was that she wanted to address over the phone, demanding that we see each other in person.

Kim came over to my house that evening. She sat down on the porch. "Paul, you should sit, too."

"Kim, what is it?"

"I'm pregnant."

"What?"

"I'm *pregnant*, Paul." She stressed that word as if it were heavy. "I'm four months along."

"Kim, I'm not trying to be rude or anything, but we haven't dated in a while. Are you sure this is my kid?"

"I'm sure, Paul. Sure as I can be. There is no doubt about it."

"OK. Well, what do you want to do? I want to do right by you, Kim," I said.

"Well I've been thinking. Don't you just want to give us a shot? Like, for *real, for the <u>sake</u> of this little one that is growing?" she said, as she pointe*d to her belly. She wasn't showing yet, but I got the point. I thought we should try for the child's sake.

This was one of my biggest mistakes because I had really strong feelings for Dolores and think she would have not given up on me like Kim did when times got tough. No regrets from the kids just the harsh treatment that I received from their mother. I still think my kids don't know the whole story of all that happen and just hope they will someday have the hart to forgive me for my weaknesses. My unconditional love for them is what almost put me in jail for years. Kim used them as a pawn to get me in trouble again and again. I think truthfully it was God who kept me from jail time and made me make the right important decisions on things that would have done me in.

WEDDING

There are more than enough shows on television today dedicated to the perfect wedding. Magazines are devoted to how to plan, and most recommend designating a year or so to get all the tasks completed. Movies glorify these events as the greatest day in the couple's life. Friends come from all over to attend parties that have grown annually more and more expensive. Well, that might be the fairy-tale wedding story. But our particular tale wasn't going to be depicted on any magazine cover any time soon.

Our wedding was a hastily arranged event. We couldn't expect much money for the wedding from Kim's family, as things were really tight for them financially. On the Ventura's side, since Dad had passed away, Mom had started to exhibit an odd combination of frugality and wasteful spending. It seemed that on this occasion, she was determined to save money. We invited about two hundred people, but Mom wanted to have the wedding and the reception at the house. It was a tight fit to say the least. I wished Dad had been there to see me get married. He would have worried, I know, that I was too young to get involved in a commitment as huge as marriage. He had often warned me that I was going to get roped in by the girls I was dating, and to be careful, to avoid getting tied down until I was older. But I know just as well that, once Kim was pregnant, Dad would have been the first to tell me to honor my responsibilities.

Neither of us wanted to have an extremely religious wedding. We were a bit different than most of the Italian Catholics in Massachusetts. We'd left the Church upon arrival in the States. I was told by my father when my father's mother came from Italy, and her husband died shortly thereafter of a heart attack, she went to the Catholic Church and told them that she was up against hard times. She lamented that she could no longer feed her kids. The Church told her that they would "pray for [her]." Immediately thereafter, my grandmother went to another church—Protestant this time—and they responded to her pleas for help with material charity. They helped her put food on her table, and she earned her religious membership as a result. Because we had left the Catholic Church, and my fiancée's family was French Protestant, our wedding was actually administered by a lady who was a justice of the peace.

The guests were mostly family. People came out of the woodwork, people I'd only heard vaguely of on the Ventura's side, and that I had never heard of on Kim's. She claimed to have never met a bunch of them, too, but I guess that is the way weddings work. All of those guests together in the same place created a stressful combination for me. I would rather have married privately and avoided the crowd. The money from the wedding gave us a good start, but I was uncomfortable with all those people wishing us well.

When Nicole was born, I had expected a boy. I just knew that this first child was going to be a boy, had even prepared the nursery in all blue. I spent a couple of days painting it robin's-egg blue and hung some boyish wallpaper border right under the molding. We went into the Malden hospital for what was a fairly standard birth. Kim labored gracefully, and after six hours, which felt like days, a beautiful girl was born. I responded with shock: "Oh my God—it's a girl!"

The doctor and nurses laughed. "Don't you know that the girl is going to love you more? And you are going to love her more than words." Apparently, a lifetime of working in the baby industry had instilled in that doctor and those nurses a little wisdom because they were as right as could be. I loved that child so much. From an early age, Nicole was a real girly girl. She loved baby dolls. She would dress them up, organize events for a group of dolls, and play house. She was also a performer. We had a little piano that she would place on the kitchen floor. She'd "play" for us on that piano and then look eagerly to us for approval. When we clapped enthusiastically, she'd glow so brilliantly. She was determined to get that approval, a determination that bled into her athletic pursuits as well. She loved soccer, took it so seriously, and tried so diligently. I just loved to watch her on the field. I did not wonder whence she got that determination. I'd felt it myself my whole life in work and play.

Two years after her birth, Nicole was introduced to her little brother. When Paul Joseph—Pauli for short—came home from the hospital, we were glad to have him safe and sound. He made it through some shaky moments during labor. When Kim and I went to the hospital, the doctor anticipated that it would be a while, since Kim wasn't dilated more than a couple of centimeters. She was going home to eat dinner and return a short time later. The nurse, after looking at the heart rate, pursed her lips and went straight to the phone. "Doctor, you better come up here."

When the OB-GYN arrived, she looked at the machines. She then turned to the nurse and proceeded to question her every competence. "Why did you call me up here? Everything looks normal."

As she said this, a different beeping pace developed. The nurse responded to the doctor's irritation. "Look!"

When the doctor looked at this machine, her face whitened. "Call downstairs."

Here I am, on pins and needles just outside the labor room, wondering what the hell is happening. As my stress continues to grow, up walks this guy in green scrubs cool as a cucumber. Later, I figured that he must have been the surgeon, up from the emergency room. I felt as if he should have been running, but he paused and looked at me as I paced. He then went to wash his hands as I walked back and forth. He motioned me toward him. "Come here. Do you already have kids?"

"Yeah. A little girl."

He responded with a level of confidence I'd never seen in my life. "Watch this. I'm going to come back in no more than two minutes, and you are going to have a son."

He went in, and I watched. I soon saw why he told me not to actually come in. The cut he made into Kim's lower belly was pretty intense. And as the blood started flowing, he pulled a blue object out of that cut. It was clear to me that there was little breath. After a couple of slaps to the bottom, and just a few minutes after the surgeon's arrival, I heard a scream the likes of which I never heard again from Pauli.

Paul Joseph played hockey. He was quick on the ice, and he seemed to have a nose for the puck. We had a certain bond. Kim would call me, when we were going through difficulties, to come put him to bed. He wouldn't go to bed without seeing Daddy. I took movies of him while we were out in the yard. I'd be doing a project, and his interest in it was something inexplicable. When I was working, he would want to act like he was working.

On one occasion in particular, we went up to Andover. That place had around two hundred units, each positioned around a central entrance. There, in late November and December, they always displayed and decorated a massive Christmas tree. That evening I'd received a call that the tree was out. I looked at the event as an opportunity to have a little adventure with my boy.

"You want to go out with Daddy and fix a tree?"

"Yeah, Dad!" he responded eagerly.

On the way up, we talked about my job, about Pauli's school, about how he was getting along with his sister. When I got there, I had a hard time figuring out why the lights on the tree were out. I tried the fuses, looked for loose cords. I searched for loose lights that might have shorted out the whole thing, but I still couldn't figure out why the lights weren't working. Finally, in my frustration, I grabbed the cords and sort of threw them down in anger. "What the hell? Why won't this tree light?"

I stormed off toward the truck, heading to get a flashlight so I could see a bit better. As I turned to get Pauli, I watched as he mimicked my gestures and words. He took the junction of the cords and pulled on them before throwing them up in the air in mock frustration. "What the hell?" he repeated. As he said it, I started formulating excuses to feed Kim about Pauli picking up on my language. But as he threw down the cords, the lights lit up. No sounds came down from the heavens. No angels appeared in full force and song. But they might as well have. Pauli looked at me, stunned, and then we went absolutely nuts.

"What did you do?"

"I don't know, Dad," he said.

"Well, I know one thing you did," I responded. "You lit the tree!"

On the drive up and back, we laughed and giggled. To this day, that remains the greatest Christmas miracle I've ever seen, and certainly the best memory of that holiday season.

But, over the years, our early affection grew more and more tepid. Benjamin Franklin once said, "Keep your eyes wide open before marriage and half shut afterwards." I think old man Franklin may have been referencing the sort of problems that developed between Kim and me. We didn't anticipate some of the difficulties we would face, and we struggled to overcome those difficulties. After all, we got married pretty young. But I remain convinced that the strains due to the greed and injustice perpetrated upon my family drove a wedge between Kim and me, which ended our marriage. That wedge would not have existed on its own, at least in the form we came to know.

When I was working for the family business, maintaining those buildings that my father had accumulated and cared for, I had a level of calm that disintegrated with the arrival of Dick Fries and Lorne Buchanan—and with their feeding frenzy on my mom.

As my stress increased over work, and over the estate stuff, Kim and I started fighting more. These fights felt all the worse given what we'd established early on. For the first few years in our marriage, things were great. I'd come home from work, and we'd eat big family dinners. We would go up to camp. We had a pool in the backyard, and her family would come over to hang out. We'd grill burgers in the yard with her parents. Her girlfriend Cathy and her sisters would come over and sip white wine while chatting in the backyard. But in retrospect, our happiness seemed to have been contingent upon money.

And when my mother's boyfriends came around, and things grew contentious with me at work, those problems bled into the house. The disagreements started small. Everything revolved around money. Kim and I took different approaches to this strain, though. I remained optimistic that I'd find something and that things would work out. She grew more and more convinced that she herself needed to find a job. The financial strains led her to start looking for work. To me, it was something of a slight. I viewed it as my job to provide, and I felt frustrated that I was struggling to find work.

We were living at the time in my family home, and that became a contentious issue as well, as all family property was under dispute in the legal battles waged across the Ventura family front. In an honest attempt to take a step back, and in an attempt to avoid a divorce for the kids' and our own sake, Kim and I decided that some time apart would perhaps catalyze some calm. But that time apart probably just made divorce feel like a more viable option.

First, she tried to move in for a while with her parents. She had gone back and forth a few times, and then they told her that she needed to make up her mind. They had no intention of endorsing this on-again, off-again routine, and they wanted her to come back to live with me for the kids' sake. Her parents and I got along well. I had, from that evening when her mom empathetically let me see Kim despite the late hour, felt that I was on good terms with Kim's mom. Plus, her dad and I had a common bond over construction. He looked to me for advice on occasion, particularly with issues of plumbing and foundational stuff. When Kim and I encountered problems after her parents booted her, she went to live with my brother Joe and his wife for a while. She'd come back home after a while, we'd get along for a couple of days, and then some bill would arrive that put us both on edge again. Kim was close with

Joe's wife, and their home was a place that felt neutral to her. Even then, though, my role as a father kept us together.

So, like I said before, Kim would often call me to come over to Joe's house to help our son go to sleep. I'd pick up Pauli at the door, as Kim didn't even want me coming into the house. That's right; I couldn't even go inside my brother's house. Still, I hadn't made a big deal about it. I just wanted to preserve my connection to the kids. So, I'd go over to Joe's and pick up little Pauli. For hours we'd ride around in my truck. He'd babble at first and talk to me about whatever was on his mind, but eventually he'd start to fade. When I saw that first yawn, I'd turn the truck back toward Joe's. And soon he was fast asleep.

Our relationship struggles continued in lockstep with the business and family controversies. After the troubles with Dick had calmed down a bit, But when the new guy—Lorne Buchanan—came into the picture, the business stopped. Our financial troubles accelerated quickly without any income from the property work.

As I struggled to scrape together an income, I had a hodge-podge of jobs. I drove an oil truck, operated dump trucks, and ran backhoes. I started cruising the advertisements in the newspaper for openings in property management work. I was thrilled for a while to get a job in Andover with a property management group. This company gave me health benefits, a decent income, and reasonable hours. And so, things with Kim went well for a while. But because I felt I could do more, I kept my eyes out for other jobs. After only six weeks with the job in Andover, I applied for and got a job offer with a management company in Wellesley. It was a great opportunity. It would have given me a chance to move up quickly and start earning more money than I had sniffed in quite some time. There was only one downside: no health benefits.

In light of that pretty glaring negative, Kim balked. I argued that I could purchase health insurance separately, but for some reason she viewed that as a riskier proposition than what I had in Andover. She wanted me to have a job with health insurance and told me that if I quit the Andover job, she was gone. I told her that I'd defer to her, though I insisted that the Wellesley job was a better gig. She remained firm in her opposition, and I ended up giving my brother Joe a recommendation for the Wellesley position. He got the job. Two to three months later, the management company in Andover was fired from the condo association. So, I went to work for my brother at the job that I could have had.

My hunt for consistent employment coincided with the settlement dispute with Mom. As Lovins dragged his feet and failed to apply for the stay, we lost even that hope for full ownership of the house. The news that the settlement offer was gone was delivered right when my wife left for good. The day we received the news, I went first to tell Kim. She was every bit as furious as I was. At that moment, I felt that we were on the same team, fighting against an intractable opposition. We talked for a few minutes, and then I went outside to find myself some busy work. I needed a task to take my mind off things, or at least to let my mind settle a bit. I had an old pickup in the yard that I was trying to fix up for work. I could see her watching me as I tried to fix it. As I caught glimpses of her in the window, I could see the frustration in her face. It was over.

When Kim moved out for good, I maintained hope regardless. I wanted to get back together for the kids' sake. I wanted my family back. I didn't hear from her for a while and didn't know where she was or with whom she had gone to stay. The Friday after she moved out—she'd left on a Monday—I heard a knock on the door. I was sitting in the living room, helping the kids do their homework, and then all of a sudden I'm holding divorce papers. I tried to be a man about it and choke back the tears. But this was a bit of a surprise. It was too much.

Divorce

After the delivery of the papers, real trouble started on the marital front. I think that Kim was looking for leverage in the divorce proceedings, but things that were previously not an issue suddenly became of great and severe moral importance. Oddly enough, right before the divorce was finalized, Kim ended up living at 976 Main Street in Melrose. This was a building that I had helped my father build, one my family owned. So, as I dropped my kids off, or came to see them, I was flooded with emotions on all fronts. I was reminded regularly of how great and ambitious my father was. But I was also reminded on those same occasions of what was happening daily to all that he'd worked for. The disrepair I noticed at 976 I took personally. I knew that if Joe and I were still involved, things would look better.

Occasionally, one of the tenants would catch me in the hall and affirm my sentiments with words of their own. "Things used to be so much better, Paul. I miss the days when I could call your dad's number and have someone respond to my problems in less than an hour. Now I have to call and call just to reach someone.

And even then, it takes a week sometimes for anything to be done about the issue."

This affirmation made me feel as if my suspicions about people trying to steal the family fortune were valid. But that validation also drove me to more and more anger. Yet, around this time, it seemed as if Kim started looking for some ammunition for the impending divorce. One day in particular, when I dropped off my kids, Nicole asked me to come in the apartment with them. Their mom wasn't going to be home for a while, and she needed some help with her homework. As I entered the kitchen, I was struck by a sickening sense of nostalgia. I had laid most of this linoleum flooring. I had put these countertops on the cabinets. As I looked over the kitchen, my eyes settled on a letter sitting on the kitchen table. I wouldn't have thought much of it, but as I glanced past it my eyes caught a name—*Ventura!* I picked it up and read that the building was now co-owned, in addition to Joseph Ventura, by Al Kendrick.

What? Dad had just died two or three years ago, and here was a change in the ownership plans for one of our buildings? Co-ownership? I called my wife at her work to ask what was happening and what the letter was all about. The substance of my questions was lost on her, though, as she was too occupied by her fury that I was in her apartment in the first place.

"Hey, Kim," I started.

"What is it, Paul?"

"Well, I've got this question," I said diplomatically.

"Yes," she said shortly.

"Well, I'm here at the building and happened to catch a name on your table. What is this letter about, Kim?"

"Where are you?" she responded.

"I'm at your place," I responded innocently, though I knew what was next.

"What the hell are you doing in my apartment?"

"Well, the kids asked me to come up. They said you weren't going to be home for a while, and they didn't want to come in alone. So I figured I'd hang with them for a bit."

"You have no right to be in there. And another question: what in the world gives you the right to read my mail?"

"I wasn't reading your mail, This is my Family's mail Kim. I just happened to catch Dad's name as I glanced at your table. It's at the top of the letter, and I saw it.

"Sure," she replied, too caught up in the bitterness of the previous months to bother figuring out whether or not I was telling the truth. "Get out of my apartment!"

"Fine, Kim. I came in because the kids asked me. But I'm leaving. I'm leaving," I responded with a voice that tried to ooze apology.

I was leaving, but it sure was hard to convince anyone I had not been up to anything malicious. In fact, my presence in her apartment that day was a huge portion of my wife's argument against me to establish a restraining order. Actually, what she worked to initiate was called an abuse prevention order, or a 209A order, from the civil courts. Other elements of this restraining order had their roots in the relationship that Kim immediately initiated, or that had been going on for some time during our marriage, with one of her co-workers at FedEx.

Before the divorce was finalized, one of my friends told me that he had seen Kim's new boyfriend Marco getting into the car that I was paying for and insuring. This guy was driving around in it like he owned the car. So, when my wife was visiting the neighbors, I went over and took the plates off the car. The police came to my house to talk about the license plates. They gave me grief, and I said I wanted to make sure Kim could get the kids from place to place. But if this guy, who had probably been the final straw in my marriage's collapse, was driving the car, I sure as hell wasn't going to insure him in the process. They backed off once they heard my explanation. Nonetheless, Kim brought it up in future legal struggles, but without the context to fully explain the situation.

Eventually, it became clear that I had been right in my feelings about this Al Kendrick guy. I know my dad would not have his name on something as co-owner. My reluctance about him was proven correct when he was arrested a couple of years later. Apparently he had defrauded someone. I would have loved to have been the person to get after him. But I had enough trouble on my hands at the time with the marriage that was eroding before my eyes. I also think they used my wife's last name living in the building to pull this scam to mail the letters to a Ventura name.

I was set up to fail with these particular restraining orders. Kim seemed determined to trick me into breaking the order, which didn't register at first. I was a bit burned by the recent scams I had put into from Kim, and I took the restraining order very seriously. Perhaps just not seriously enough to anticipate the ways she would try to get me to break it. I was, in hindsight, sort of easy prey. Most of her success came from leveraging my desire to see the kids. On each of those occasions, I was surprised to hear from her but so excited to see the kids that I abandoned wisdom and my best judgment.

More specifically to the facts, as became all too frequently the case with us, I received a letter from her lawyer that read the following:

Kimberly will be out of the Commonwealth for a while. She has won an all-expense-paid vacation with her employer, FedEx. Would you like to keep the kids?

I didn't think much about the rationale of this letter. What it asked was a no-brainer for me. Of course I wanted to spend some time with the kids. But it didn't actually happen that way. The times that Kim had chosen for me to keep them conflicted with my current work schedule. It was the worst of times to ask for time off, too, as I needed the money badly and had been hired on a sort of trial basis. So, Kim actually had her mother keep the kids. I kept them on my normal times, but not much more than that.

But because I'd received that letter, I was not surprised to hear from Kim on the day that she was supposed to return. She'd run into some travel difficulties and was not going to get back home on time. I believe that her flight had been delayed. When she called to ask if I could help out and go pick up the kids, I figured that, since I had been invited to stay with the kids and asked by Kim to go pick them up, I should be OK. No such luck.

When I got to the YMCA, I tried to check out the kids. The lady at the desk claimed that I was not on the list. I was sympathetic with her. She was obviously just trying to do her job and protect the children in her care. But I had been told to pick up Nicole and

Pauli. So, I sat in the lobby area to wait on this woman to check me out in more detail. She said that she was going to "try to call someone in the family." But, apparently, the only thing she did was call the cops.

All of a sudden, a policeman walked in. He approached me without haste but with a no-nonsense demeanor. "Mr. Ventura, what is going on?"

I was stressed that he knew my name because that was a pretty good sign that I could expect some trouble. I didn't know this guy at all. Nonetheless, I responded with my best calm voice. "Oh, just trying to pick up the kids. I was told to come and get them."

He grimaced just a bit as I said this, and I knew what he'd been told to expect. "No, you can't do that. You aren't on the list. Your ex-wife's sister has already gotten them, and you aren't allowed to pick them up in the first place."

I doubted that he'd believe me anyway, so I decided not to make much of a scene. So, I just responded as affably as I could. "OK, no big deal. I must have misunderstood."

But on my way home, I happened upon a car that I recognized. The babysitter lived right up the road from me, so it was not the coincidence it appears to be. But as I drove by the sitter's house and saw Kim's car in the driveway, I pulled over. My kids were in the car hanging out of the window. Kim was not there, so I asked the kids who had picked them up. When they told me it was Jill, I told them to call me when they get a chance.

Kim was up to her old tricks again, and once again I fell for it. In the police report that she would soon fill out, Kim claimed that I had followed her to the police station. I didn't, but if I'd wanted to see the police, I didn't have to wait long. Within an hour, the police showed up at my house.

Once they arrived at my door the police asked that I come outside with them. I didn't want them to arrest me, but when I expressed that concern, they promised, "All we want to do is talk." I once again sought solace in the fact that I'd done absolutely nothing wrong. *OK*, I thought, *they can't lie to me. I'll just stand on the porch and talk to them if that is what they want.* Big mistake! As soon as I walked out the door, two of the policemen grabbed me by my arms. I resisted a bit verbally and tried to pull back into the house as they ripped me away from my door.

"What are you guys doing? Stop it! I thought we were just going to talk. My wife wasn't even there at the time, and the restraining order does not extend to the kids. What have I done wrong?"

As I clinched my arms, they threw me down on the ground. The other policeman aimed something at my face and clinched his finger. The next thing I knew, the whole world had gone white. My face felt like it was on fire. I couldn't open my eyes, and about ten seconds after they sprayed me, I started to have difficulty breathing. It felt like my airways were shutting down. My eyes started watering, and I couldn't see much of anything.

"Jesus. What in the world did I do to deserve that?"

"Should have come peacefully," they'd responded (a bit too happily if you ask me).

"I did respond peacefully," I said, exasperated. "I walked outside. God almighty!"

"Should have stayed away from your ex-wife."

By this point, the burning had reached a new level of pain. I couldn't even think straight, and when I tried to stand, I had to actually sit back down. My muscles in my lower body wouldn't even work because of the pain in my eyes, nostrils, and on my face, in general. I'd heard that by blinking, you start to wash the stuff out of your eyes. But every time I blinked, it felt as if my eyes were absorbed in a fire hotter than hell.

The policemen told me that if I requested that the ambulance guy, who was standing near the booking station, clean my face, they were going to charge me with resisting arrest. If I didn't request to be cleaned, they would just charge me with breaking the restraining order. How the choice was reasonable was beyond me. Meanwhile, the ambulance guy was standing to the side of the desk laughing. What kind of human beings was I dealing with, to be laughing at another person's misery?

Then, one of the cops escorted me to Cell Eight.

"Hey," he said. "We'll start calling that Paul's cell, huh?"

I was mute. I figured that talking to these people had done me little good. In addition, since I hadn't been allowed to even wash my face, the effects of the spray had hardly abated. In fact, the difficulties I'd faced earlier in breathing were getting worse and worse. Any attempt I made to get some help was met with scoffing and laughter. I begged one of the officers for help. "Hey, please I can't breathe in here. I need some help."

I was banging on the Plexiglas, and one of the policemen came to see what I was doing.

"Can't do anything for you," the cop responded.

My wheezing grew worse and worse until my world went black. I really thought I was going to die that night. I even put my head in my shirt to help me breath and that was the last thing I remember I blacked out. The next thing I knew, someone I'd never seen before was leaning over me. "Wake up, sir. Time for your day in court."

When I arrived at the courthouse, the cops who had talked a great deal about resisting arrest apparently stuck to their word. At least they had a speck of decency. But how was that resisting arrest anyway? Of course I wasn't going to take what they did to me passively. Who did they think I was, Gandhi? When I struggled against them, I was simply trying to get them to stop beating the hell out of me. I wasn't resisting anything except for the pain and discomfort they were so effectively administering. They should have at least given me the opportunity to tell my side of the story of what really happen.

After that weekend, and my first run-in with the police following the restraining order, I got to know, a bit too well for my own liking, a guy named Steve Anzalone. He was my probation officer. Movies often depict cops or detectives as intense in their focus on a particular criminal. On *Law & Order*, cops often threaten "preps" and tell them that they are going to "know what [the prep] is eating, when they are sleeping." Well, some detectives really do have that go-getter spirit. But the most intense person I'd ever met in law enforcement was this probation officer. He was a tall, heavyset guy whose curly hair on the sides of his head tried to make up for the lack thereof on top. He had one of those old tough-guy looks, and whenever he cut those steely eyes at me, I grew nervous. For the year after that initial restraining order, he was absolutely up my ass.

The worst was that much of what Steve required of me was contradictory. He required that I had a job and proved that I was earning an income. This way, he could make sure that I could meet one dimension of my requirements in the divorce—child support. But he also required that I meet him at two o'clock once a week. Well, that time happened to conflict pretty heavily with my job, but he was having none of my explanations of the difficulties this posed.

"Mr. Anzalone, I can't be at work and with you at the same time. I am going to lose my job. I haven't had it long enough to ask for all that time off during the peak work hours."

"What I don't want from you is excuses. I don't give a shit about that. Make it happen."

Then he gave me a surrender letter, which meant that he was going to give me up to the judge for not abiding by my probation if I failed to show for my next meeting with him.

At one point, I went to the courthouse in the landscaping truck from work. I went to see my probation officer, and for that reason, I almost got fired the next morning. As I stormed into the courthouse, leaving the truck running, I came into his office and began shouting.

"I'm here! I left all the guys in Arlington, and I'm probably going to get fired from taking the truck from them."

Then he decided to revoke the surrender letter. It seemed that perhaps he was softening in his perception of me. He even went before the judge and told him that I'd satisfied his expectations.

My feelings had little to do with my fate, though. I still had to go into his office to meet with him. Then, on random occasions, I'd have to take drug tests. On the day that he made me go take the test, I told him that I'd walk as quickly as I could, but that I didn't think I'd make it on time. After all, I didn't have a car. I struck out nonetheless, comforted at least that I'd taken the full day off from work. I still doubted that I'd arrive at the health office in time. Next thing I knew, after about half a mile of walking, up pulls this little pickup truck. It was Mr. Anzalone. "Get in!" he shouted.

That was perhaps the turnaround point. I knew now that he was on my side.

Even Mr. Anzalone's strict watch and his regulations couldn't keep me from messing up given Kim's anger and insistence on tricking me into breaking the restraining order. The second time this happened, I received a call from my son, Pauli.

"Hey, Dad. You coming to my hockey game on Saturday?"

"Ah…I'd love to, son. But I can't. You know I can't. Your mom has that paper out against me that says I'm not allowed."

"I know, Dad. But she told me that she'd lifted it."

"She what?"

"Yeah, I begged her, and she told me that she'd lift it so you can see my games."

The next day I received a paper telling me that there was no restraining order, so I felt safe going to the game. I also felt that Pauli's call and words made a great deal more sense. It was a mystery to me why she had lifted the restraining order, but I actually experienced a great deal of excitement as I headed over to the Medford Hockey Rink. I always loved seeing Pauli play sports! When I arrived, caution prevailed, and perhaps saved me in retrospect because I decided to sit on the visitors' side of the rink—even though I knew my son's team was the home side for this game. I wanted to make sure I gave Kim all the space she needed. That caution was all for naught, though, and I certainly should have heeded that reluctant feeling in the pit of my stomach as I contemplated going to the game. As soon as I eased up to the boards alongside the ice to watch the game, two cops showed up and stood on either side of me.

"Don't create a scene," one of them whispered forcefully. "Get up and follow us outside."

"Don't create a scene? What do you mean? I'm just here watching my son play hockey."

"We all know that you aren't supposed to be here. Get up and come out with us."

We walked to the foyer where the concession stand was, and I expected that once there they'd give me a chance to tell my side of the story. I even took out the paper that I'd received in the mail.

"Here, look at this!" I said to them, sure that they would listen to me with a legal document in my hands. The document said plainly and simply that the order had been lifted. No such luck. They asked no questions. They looked at it haphazardly and muttered, "There must have been another one."

Afterward, they just issued imperatives. "Put your hands behind your back."

"You are cuffing me? I was told to come here by my son. He told me that Kim had lifted the order."

"Hands behind your back, sir."

So, they cuffed me and put me in a cruiser. Then, they locked me up for what would turn into a long weekend in jail. They took me to Medford and processed me, and then the Melrose police picked me up to take me to their place. When I finally got a moment in court, after that long weekend, the judge began with an invitation.

"Mr. Ventura, tell me why you believe you are here unfairly."

When I explained my situation, that I'd gone into the game based on the belief that the restraining order had been lifted, and I stood on the opposite side of the rink to stay clear of her, and that I'd had legal documentation on my very person to prove that the order had been lifted, the judge grew more and more aghast.

"There is no way you should even be here right now. That isn't legal. And can you tell me why you went from Medford to Melrose and then to court in Somerville? I don't even have jurisdiction here. Case dismissed."

Despite this judge's frustration with the proceedings, I wasn't out of the woods. The third strike came again under similarly dubious circumstances. It seemed to have arisen from a combination of me saying something that was not allowed and/or me calling Kim at times that weren't appropriate. On the first front, I received a call a short time after the incident at the hockey rink occurred from someone who sounded official.

"Mr. Ventura?"

"This is him."

I'm calling from Wakefield Elementary School. We haven't seen Nicole in a while. We haven't been able to reach Mrs. Ventura."

"You mean 'Kim,' and she isn't 'Mrs. Ventura' anymore."

"Well, do you know anything about why Nicole hasn't been at school? She has been out for three days."

"I don't have a clue. But I'll try to find out and let you know."

I had a pretty good idea where I could find Nicole. Kim and one of our neighbors had become best friends, and her name was Kim also. She was babysitting the kids up the street from my house. When I walked outside, I happened to see my daughter, Nicole.

I yelled from the front of my house out to her: "Nicole, why haven't you been at school?"

"Oh hey, Dad! What are you doing?"

"Right now I'm worried about the fact that you are skipping school. Why are you doing that?"

"I've been taking care of Grandma."

"Well, there is no reason for you to miss school. That is the most important thing. You have to tell your mother that she needs to find someone else to take care of Grandma because they are calling and wondering where you are."

"OK, Dad. I'll tell her. No problem."

But it turned out to be a problem because as soon as I got back to my house, the doorbell rang. When I reached the window to look and see who it was, I saw three policemen. Then I looked to the street and saw three cruisers, blue lights flashing.

I thought why in hell are they here know?. But then I was comforted by another thought: *I haven't done anything malicious or wrong.* So I cracked the door.

"What can I do for you, gentlemen?"

"Why don't you come outside, sir?"

I wasn't going to do it. I felt uneasy with the looks on their faces, and the last time I'd responded to a request like this from policemen, I'd found myself in handcuffs and in the back of a police car.

"Can you please come outside, sir?" they asked a bit more emphatically. They added, "We just want to talk. Come out and tell us your story."

I did. Jail it was. Again.

Due to the terms of this order, and Steve Anzalone recommendations, I was going to be due for a trial date. I dreaded it and hated that it had come to this. How had Kim so quickly gone from a loving wife to someone railroading me, someone clearly hell-bent on getting me thrown in jail? I knew that I had better be prepared for the worst, as she clearly wasn't constrained by little things like honesty or integrity. She would do anything to get her way, and I started to gear up for my responsibility to do likewise.

The lawyer who worked on the restraining order infractions was a guy named Carroll Ayers, whom I've previously mentioned. He'd done the work on my divorce case. I'd been relatively pleased with him throughout that process and didn't want to make any changes. Later, I began to seriously doubt that decision. As he mocked some of my fears and demonstrated a total lack of empathy for my plight, I wondered whether or not switching horses midstream would have actually resulted in anything worse than working with Carroll. Hindsight is twenty-twenty, but this guy certainly didn't seem to have my best interest buried in the depths of his heart. I wonder, in fact, why he took the case, other than sheer greed.

TRIAL

Inside Cambridge Superior Courthouse in Central Square, we waited for our case to come up on the docket. As was per usual in these circumstances, I found my palms sweaty and muscles antsy. I struggled to keep still.

When our case was called, we made our way to the front of the court. The judge spent a few minutes reading through the various briefs and paperwork. He gave Carroll and the district attorney their respective opportunities to speak. Both said a few things about the facts of the case.

After they spoke, the judge looked to me, paused, and then said in a voice both grave and self-satisfied, "I'm going to give you the deal of the century today. I'm going to let you leave today, but if you get into any trouble, you are going straight to jail. There will be no trial."

My mind raced. I wasn't convinced that what the judge was offering was in my best interest. After the previous months, I doubted that a future without any police interaction was even remotely possible. I had been as diligent and careful as I could be to follow the requirements of the restraining order, and I still found myself standing here in court. So I responded, "I'm not taking it."

The judge glanced up from his documents, surprised. He looked to my lawyer. "You want to take a few minutes to talk to your client?"

"Yes, your honor."

Carroll and I went out into the hallway, where he encouraged me to take the deal. He was more scared of the judge than I was.

"You need to take this deal, Paul," he said.

"I'm not taking it."

"You just don't understand," he said to me with a mixture of urgency and frustration. "You need to take it. A trial might not go well for you. Typically men who are accused of this sort of thing find it difficult to elicit any sympathy from a jury. Kim will look a great deal more innocent than you."

"No way," I responded. "I didn't even do the things they are accusing me of. What is to stop them from making up more lies?"

Carroll looked less than satisfied, but we made our way back into the courtroom nonetheless to tell the judge the news. "Your honor" my client refuse the offer, and the judge once again ordered us outside again. This time, we went in the corner near some old drink machines. Carroll begged me, "Paul, you have to take this. There isn't any choice."

"Carroll, I am not taking it. There is no way."

Back in the courtroom, the judge looked really frustrated but said very little else to dissuade us.

"You'll be on trial in a couple of weeks. Do you understand the decision you just made?"

"I do, your honor."

"Do you understand that if you lose in this trial, you will most likely spend two to three years out in the state jail in Walpole?"

I grimaced a bit as that reality sank in, but I responded with another, "Yes, your honor."

I was scared, but I knew that all of the stuff that had been levied against me was totally bogus. What was to protect me from simi-lar lies in the future? I knew that if I got a group of fair people as a jury, then Kim would have no shot of proving that I had been anything other than reasonable with regard to the order. I also hoped that, after this trial, my slate would be clean.

In the weeks leading up to the trial, despite my firm belief in my own innocence, I hardly slept, if at all. I bounced around my house like a lunatic. At times I figured that I had been set up, and that I was going away for sure. At other times, I had a bit more optimism about the judgment of my fellow man. I was innocent and had gotten my day in court. What did I have to fear?

But the good days were rare. On most days, I was a blend of paranoid and depressed—a total train wreck. The snows had arrived in New England, bringing with them repressive and constant cold. No one wanted to go outside, but no matter where I went, I couldn't find shelter from the psychological cold and doubt that plagued me. I could barely breathe for stress over the past. In the weeks of preparation before we went to trial, money began to be more of an issue for Carroll. In an effort to raise money to pay him, I'd been trying to sell an old Cadillac my neighbor Mr. Forgione had given me. This was the car I took the license plates off when Kim had her boyfriend driving the car she gave it back to me .It was old but was in the kind of immaculate shape that only retirees have time to manage. It was a four-door, brown 1980s Coupe de Ville. The interior was tan, and if there were no stains or markings on it, I never saw a cleaner car.

So, as Carroll kept asking me for money, I began to try more and more earnestly to sell that car. Finally, after weeks of discussion, he persuaded me to just give him the car and the title for payment. He had plans to take it with him down to his vacation place in Florida. Resolving that money issue granted me very little reprieve when it came to the stress of the pending trial, though.

The trial was set in Cambridge. For legal reasons beyond me, the judge in Malden had determined that Cambridge Court had primary legal jurisdiction over the case. The day of the trial, I woke up early, showered, and put on my best clothes. I knew what was expected of me regarding appearance at these sort of things. I drove the thirty minutes on Interstate 93 and then got off on Mystic Avenue. The time couldn't go slowly enough for me. Though I had no doubt about my innocence, I dreaded the possibility that some jurors would not share my surety. I sat in the parking garage and thought to myself: *If I am found guilty, who will take care of my bills? What about my truck in the parking garage? Why haven't I made any arrangements? Please god not guilty!*

Nonetheless, I arrived all too quickly at the courthouse. I walked into the gray cobblestone building right off Central Square in Cambridge. It was a mostly concrete building, like one of those eighties high-rises. I knew the place well, as I'd spent the weekend there after one of the restraining order problems.

The first day was the jury selection. One of Carroll's big points early on was the importance of picking primarily men for the jury. His theory was that men tended to side with men, and that women will almost always side with women. But I had a different theory. I knew that my wife was trying to railroad me out of anger. I knew that she was essentially trying to manipulate the legal system for her own benefit. Who better to understand those motivations and intentions than a fellow woman? Against Carroll's advice, I picked all women and two men for the jury. As I selected each one, he grimaced and muttered to me, "What are you doing? This is so stupid."

"It is my life on the line here. I know what I want."

Unlike the divorce proceedings, which had been lower stress Carroll and I started to very quickly develop a bit of a contentious relationship. In matters of the trial, I felt that he consistently ignore my wishes.

The first portion of the trial was opening arguments during which the DA attempted to establish a variety of accusation against me. She said that I'd relentlessly tried to contact Kim, despite the restraining order. She said that I'd threatened her and shown up where I shouldn't have. But she also said that some of my actions had brought danger to the children. At the last part, my anger reached a near-boiling point, and I struggled to restrain myself.

The first person called to the stand in the trial was Kim. Right off the bat, her lawyer led her through a series of questions about a firearm that I supposedly kept in the bedroom closet.

"What about your ex-husband's behavior, specifically, scared you?" the lawyer asked, setting her up.

"Well, on one occasion, I found a gun in our bedroom closet. I believe it was loaded."

At this statement I totally lost it, jumping up and shouting, "She is trying to set me up! I am getting framed here." I knew that if they thought that I actually had a firearm, it would be an immediate jail sentence due to the terms of the restraining order.

The judge struck his gavel as Carroll grabbed me and pulled me to the seat. "Sit down, Paul! You can't do that."

"She is trying to set me up! It isn't my gun!"

After explaining the situation to Carroll, led Kim through a series of questions on cross-examination that undermined her accusation about the gun.

"Mrs. Ventura," he started out, "do you know when my client bought this gun?"

"No, I don't."

"Did he, to your knowledge, ever buy this gun?"

I watched anxiously to see what Kim's answer would be. It would tell me a great deal about what lengths she'd go to for victory. Would she perjure herself?

I breathed a slight sigh of relief when she responded with an honest answer.

"No."

"Mrs. Ventura, to whom did this gun belong originally?"

"My brother," Kim responded reluctantly.

He continued to question her, and he finally drew from her that I had not ever even known about the gun. Her brother Robbie had come over with it one day to kill a squirrel that had gotten into the house. Why in the world they felt that it would be reasonable to shoot a squirrel inside is beyond me. Regardless, he'd left it in my closet, and when I found the gun getting dressed for work one day, I was absolutely furious. I had never been much for guns anyway, and there were kids in this house. My kids! What if they had found it? What if something bad had happened?

Through undermining Kim's accusation about the gun, my case got off to a really positive start. Kim had come across in the jury's initial assessment as dishonest, or at least capable of putting forward varieties of the truth that warranted further inspection.

It was clear from the get-go that she was willing to do almost any-thing to screw me over, a first impression I'd hoped would stick with those female jurors.

Not everything that the prosecution tried to establish was as boldly false. They went through phone records, noting that I'd made a significant number of phone calls. The number in ques-tion—I can't recall exactly how many there were—the prosecution argued was egregious. Of course, many of those calls had been logistical. I'd called Kim's apartment to figure out who was to pick up the kids and when. At times I'd returned her calls upon her very own request. The prosecution neglected to mention these facts. He focused simply on the number of calls in the evening, arguing that calling Kim had been forbidden in the restraining order.

When we got to spin our own particular version of the truth, turns out we could answer to all of the prosecution's accusations. One time, in particular, Kim called me to ask about the kids, whom I had over the weekend. Our call was dropped (frankly, I think she hung up on me) and, after I didn't hear from her for a while, I called her back. We had yet to agree to a couple of logisti-cal details, and I needed to ask her a couple of more questions. This was the kind of thing for which I was being criticized here in court. This was just one example, but I had an explanation for all of those events. Upon Carroll's cross-examination and investi-gation into the call times, it became clear that an overwhelming number of the calls had been made between six and seven in the evening. That window had been specifically allowed so I could talk with the kids. So, many of the supposed infractions were actually a sign of how serious I took the order. I felt, and surely I was biased, that I was winning. Carroll didn't share my optimism. He continu-ally treated me as if he thought I was guilty. I don't know if he was mad about the money issues I'd faced, or because I'd refused to take his advice on the makeup of the jury that now sat before us.

On day two of the trial, Kim's lawyer read letters that I had writ-ten to her. Most I'd written before the restraining order was estab-lished, so I wondered how they were relevant. In them, from the depths of my heart, I begged Kim to take me back for our sake and for the sake of the kids. I was most worried that, if the marriage fully dissolved, I would lose my role as a father as well. These pleas, which had come from a private and personal place in my heart, were painted in this courtroom as a sign of my intransigence, my inability to move on. They were used to depict a sort of lunatic that couldn't take no for an answer. Carroll did a nice job of articulating that the letters might also show a loving and husbandly affection. They were not necessarily the work of someone stubborn. In short, he turned the meaning of them into a positive testament to my goodness.

To establish that I had a temper, Kim's lawyer mentioned my taking the plates off the car after I found out her boyfriend had been driving it. I began to feel more and more confident. If this was the best evidence they had of a temper, what kind of case did they have? I mean, who would continue to pay insurance on a car that their ex-wife's new boyfriend was driving? If the jury couldn't understand that action as reasonable, I didn't necessarily think I wanted to be called sane. At least not their type of sane.

Despite my burgeoning confidence, it wasn't the easiest thing in the world to sit in a public place while strangers—and the former love of my life—picked apart my character and attacked my decency as a father and husband. I wanted to stand and shout about my innocence, raise my voice to defend my honor. At the very least, and on the legal front, I wanted to take the stand myself. Carroll insisted that this wasn't a good idea. He thought that the lawyers would try to get me tricked up and confused, and that my emotional state would lead me to be susceptible to such manipulation. My desire to clear my name could hardly overcome the strength of his rationale. I knew he was right, in particular because I was so tired. I must have looked like a zombie. And during the entire trial, my heart was racing . How could that be? And what would happen to that heart if I was the center of Kim's lawyers' efforts to mislead the jury?

The goal of Kim's team grew more clear as the questions to Kim continued. They were trying to argue that Kim had undergone a long history of mental and verbal abuse. Had we had our fights? Sure. We were just like any married couple in that regard.

I've mentioned how the fights accelerated as the level of financial stress and strain intensified. But if I was guilty of verbal threats and mental abuse, she was certainly guilty as well. Our fights were *not* one-sided affairs.

She claimed, on one occasion, that I had choked her with a phone cord. On the night in question, she had called the cops. When they arrived, they found no signs of any violence. But what they did find was a shattered coffee cup. After all, the only violence that those walls had seen that evening came from a Roger Clemens–style toss of a full coffee cup, courtesy of Kim, at my head. So when both versions of that story came to light, I started to hope more and more that the jury would have very little upon which to base a conviction.

Nonetheless, it was really difficult to hear her particular version of events that were true. That we were so far from each other now that we saw events so differently was really hard for me to take. I was heartbroken as I heard her speak and saw her attempts to draw blood. She was so pissed. My efforts to repair our relationship had proved clairvoyant. I worried we would reach a depth that we didn't know we had. But this was even worse than I'd dreamed. *Look at where my life went,* I thought. *Look at where hers went. We had been living a dream. We had beautiful and loving kids.* And then, when trouble arose with Dick and Lorne, I could suddenly no longer offer her what I wanted or expected. She could hardly have been less empathetic.

All in all the trial lasted three days. They were without question the longest three days of my life. The final day was essentially set aside for closing arguments and jury deliberation. During the closing arguments, I was shocked. It seemed Carroll really and truly cared. I was mystified. He had acted like a total jackass to me for days, nay weeks. But then, he really turned on the emotional intensity. I still don't know if that emotional empathy he displayed for me that day was real or just professional skill. Whatever the roots of his display, I was grateful. After all, I was staring at three years in jail if I lost.

The prosecutor, in her own closing statement, attempted to portray me as villainous. I felt confident, though, that after two full days of defense, and after airing my own side of the story, the jury could not possibly view me as the monster that the prosecution insinuated I was.

Perhaps Carroll was convinced because as the jury walked out, he leaned over and whispered to me, "See you in three years, Paul."

His lack of professionalism in that moment had no time to sink in. I had no time to worry because I was too busy looking at the jury as they filed back into the courtroom. My attention went directly to those women's faces. I figured that, if they had voted to convict me, they wouldn't want to look me in the face. Because of the way the room was set up, I was seated right next to the jury box. I was on the right side of the room, and the jury box was on the right as well. Carroll's words echoed faintly in my ears as I looked to the first woman, the forewoman of the jury, holding the envelope in her left hand. She looked me directly in the eyes. She didn't flinch. As the rest of them filed in, I looked at them each in turn. They all met my gaze.

"Madame forewoman, have you reached a verdict?"

"We have, your honor," she responded.

The judge then took the document from her and read it. His face gave away nothing. I'd hate to see him at the poker tables with that lack of emotion! The judge passed it back to the leader of the jury, and she read the verdict: "We, the jury, find the defendant not guilty on all counts."

Before she'd even finished that word "not," I started celebrating. "Yes! I knew it! Thank you!" I screamed at the ceiling and the world but was quickly chastised by Carroll.

"Paul, don't do that. Calm down."

"Calm down?" I responded. "What are you saying? They said 'not guilty.'"

"Yeah," he responded with little celebration in his voice, "but you can't be so loud."

"I can leave, right? I can leave?" I responded, immune to his lack of excitement and full of my own.

"Yeah, you can leave," he replied.

I realize now that he cared very little for the amount of joy I was feeling at the time. What kind of lawyer doesn't care that his or her clients are happy, by the way?

"Thanks, man!" I said to him, forgetful in my joy of how little he'd had to do with the success.

When I got home, I got out of my truck and started dancing. The girl who was renting the top room in my house heard me and came out to check on me as I ran around dancing in the yard.

"What is the matter?" she asked, obviously thinking that something had gone seriously wrong with me.

"Nothing at all," I responded, though not necessarily answering the meaning behind her words. I continued, "I've just been found not guilty. I've been in court, but now I'm home. And I can tell you the first thing I'm doing: I'm going to sleep!"

"Congrats!"

"Thanks! You can't know how great this feels."

A couple of days later, I went to see Mr. Anzalone. He smiled as I walked through the door. "Congratulations on the victory in trial. How does it feel?"

"How do you think I feel? Like a million bucks, man!" As I said this, my whole face glowed with the excitement of having been validated.

"Paul, I've got to tell you that you've got guts," he said to do what you did.

"Mr. Anzalone, it has nothing to do with guts. I just knew that I was in the right." And I did. I appreciated that he was trying to pay me a compliment, but I wanted to preserve the validity of the verdict, too. I wasn't just gutsy. I was right!

"Well, you were right to stick to your guns, then. I'm proud of you.

As he said this, I could indeed see pride in his eyes. I felt proud to have earned his praise.

Mom's Death

Around this time, even amid the successes of my legal battles, Mom's health really took a turn for the worse. She developed a leaky mitral valve. This is the valve that keeps blood from flowing back into the lungs. When it starts leaking—the medical phrase is called *mitral valve prolapse*—repair is generally agreed to be the only option, as neglecting the leak dramatically increases the chances of heart attack and heart disease.

This was the moment that Mom's destructive habits finally caught up with her. She had been in and out of the hospital for years, and her emphysema was getting worse. A doctor told her at one point, "If you don't stop drinking, you will be dead in two years." After hearing this, she should have tried to stop drinking and smoking. But Mom didn't have the same support she had when Dad was alive.

Recommendations from the doctor were to quit drinking and quit smoking. Period. End of story. One doctor tried to get her to shape up. He was blunt about the consequences if she failed to do this. Her heart operation hadn't changed a thing in her behaviors.

Lorne didn't care. Or, he claimed that he couldn't do much to stop her. Dad had smoked for years as well, but he tried to recruit Mom in his attempts to quit. He had a hard time doing so, and they would try to encourage each other to knock it off. That was the difference. Dad tried to bring out the best in Mom. When she got too drunk, or went too far off the rails, he'd take her into detox centers. We would not see her for a few weeks. "Mom is sick," he'd say, "but we are going to make her better." When she came back, she would in fact be a different person.

Lorne did not encourage Mom's best habits. It was hard for us to see it all because they spent a great deal of time farther north. They stayed often at our camp in New Hampshire, and Mom started to be more and more in and out of hospitals. She was on so many different medications. I was getting all the information I had from my sisters, particularly Edy. She went toe to toe with Lorne; she wanted Mom to get help and tried to convince him of the same. She had no luck.

At Mom's funeral, it was hard for me to keep my cool. Lorne was there. My sisters and brother were there. Lorne's friends were there as well as people whom we'd never met before. Butler Funeral Home was located in a little house on Albion Street, right down the street from our office. It was, in general, a service that I couldn't get into. Here I was at Mom's funeral surrounded by strangers who wanted my family's money. What the hell was I supposed to do in the face of that level of frustration?

After the service, they took her to a cemetery in Antrim, New Hampshire. I had long-term memories of driving past that place and thinking about how old it was, how old the tombstones were. New England, because it has been settled for the longest, has some cemeteries with gravestones that you can barely read. Her sisters arranged for her to be buried up near our camp. She was supposed to be buried with my father in Wakefield at Forest Glades. He bought a site for his whole family, and it was enough space for eight people. He anticipated that Mom would be buried there. But when Dad died, Mom didn't get him a gravestone. She just added on to the bottom of his mother's, with his name and date. I thought it was odd at the time, but there was no rationalizing with her. In retrospect, that should have been my first clue that Mom's memory of Dad was washing away in a sea of vodka.

During the years after our lawsuit, the girls had still been friendly with Mom. Edy had been in the hospital frequently with Mom and had been the caregiver for her. She always checked in to figure out what was happening. I don't know how Edy had the time to do all this, as she was the mother of three boys herself. She had to battle through Lorne to find out anything. He was a road-block when she tried to find information, telling her that it was "none of her business" and that "he was taking care of things." Edy insisted, "You aren't taking care of her. You need to help her help herself on the health front."

Edy was able to manage Lorne's shenanigans a bit more calmly than I. He drove me away from Mom because I often worried that I couldn't control myself when around him. The night Mom died, Edy called me to tell me that Mom was near her end. I'd heard this frequently before, as she'd been so regularly in and out of the hospital. My girlfriend, Maria, who would later be the mother of my son, Mateo, encouraged me to go, but I was worried that Lorne might be there. If he was there, I knew that I'd absolutely blow a gasket. I couldn't control myself around this guy at the time.

When I think back, the biggest moment in the dissolution of the family business happened when Mom was too sick to think much about her actions. In a legal deposition, Lorne said that for the couple of years leading up to her death, Mom was drinking three to five drinks a day. If that number is correct, then every one of them was a triple, and he made sure that they were tall enough. A couple of months before Mom passed in 1998, she and Lorne went into her lawyer's office to have the will redrawn. We didn't know this was happening, but the results had a dramatic effect on all of us.

The family was cut out, and Lorne got everything. Go figure. That the attorney believed to have drawn up my mother's prenuptial when she married was now prepared to change it from the children to my mother's new husband. This was done only a short time before my mother's death. This woman was almost always drunk during this time, was on numerous medications that were not supposed to be taken with alcohol, and, toward the end of her life, was toting around an oxygen tank as she puffed on cigarettes. In this new will, which we found out about after Mom died, even the girls and grandchildren had been cut. Lorne claimed to have been surprised by this as well, but then he was there when the new document was signed.

In the weeks that followed Mom's death, Lorne had a real estate guy named Chris Barrett give estimates on the various properties. Right after Mom's death, some land in Wakefield sold for $270,000. That was the piece of land that, in the original settlement agreement, I had with my mother I was supposed to get. There was no mortgage on that land, so that went straight into Lorne's pocket, post-taxes. He also sold our camp we built that took us years of hard labor in New Hampshire.

We received some small snippet of the life insurance policy Mom had taken out years ago, before Lorne entered the picture. The girls, my sisters, approached Lorne in various stages of anger and frustration. Diana had a moment when she yelled at him, and Edith Ann and Marianne both tried to talk some reason into him. He then sent a letter to all of us attempting to assuage some of that anger. He claimed that the girls would get gifts of $10,000 each from the sale of that property in Wakefield, so long as there was no litigation. Here was this guy, who now had the keys to a million-dollar empire. He'd just made $270,000 by selling some property our father had bought years earlier, and he thought that extending a promise of $10,000 gifts would calm the Ventura children down. And it was a tepid promise at best. One of my favorite lines was, "Although it is always difficult to predict exactly what the future will hold, this letter is sent to each of you as a good faith outline of what Lorne would like to do if he is financially able."

Lorne later admitted legally that his intentions to include the daughters in the estate were limited to the sale of that property in Wakefield. In other words, that would be it. Well, although the future might be a bit unclear, certain elements of that future were crystal clear. Dad had always talked about the fact that property is always valuable, and we had plenty of that. We knew that, no matter what the future might hold, it certainly held a degree of financial stability if things were managed right.

The letter made some vague threats as well: "If you have litigation, and a great deal of money would have to be spent for lawyers, it would make it very difficult for Lorne to proceed with the long-range goals he currently has contemplated for each of you."

When our lawyers asked for some specificity about what those goals might be, he offered absolutely no specifics. And the way that this letter lorded over us his control of the money was just too much.

So in 1998 Lorne's lawyer, Rick Plouffe, who had also written up the prenuptial agreement that should have prevented this in the first place, filed a petition of probate to recognize the latter will, executed on May 12, 1997. And about a year later, my sisters all filed what was called an "appearance in objection to the allowance of the will." Essentially, they wanted to contest it. Joe and I got involved as well, filing our affidavits of objection a couple of months later.

Shortly thereafter, Plouffe tried to have those motions and affidavits struck, as we had taken more than the allotted time to submit them. That was denied, and the courts gave us one hundred days to collect information in the discovery process. It was during this process that we finally began to see the true depth of what Lorne had been doing, and just how far under his thumb Mom had been.

Lorne claimed that the mortgages on the property were over-extended, and that, when the economy sunk around 1990, the business had gone into the red. As a result of that, the liquidation of assets really began. Mom sold everything in Florida, including some restaurant that none of her children ever even knew she'd been involved with.

In that deposition, Lorne attributed the significant decline in the value of the estate—which had occurred, by the way, while he was around—to "mismanagement and other factors." Well, who was managing things? Mom was too drunk to stand, much less to read and sign documents, make decisions regarding properties, and run the day-to-day operations.

* * *

In 1997, Great Britain officially gave back control of Hong Kong to the Chinese. This ended close to 150 years of foreign rule, giving China control of this island country that had been signed over in the height of Britain's imperial domination. These days, British citizens look back at that time with a degree of shame. What gave them the right to make money off the backs of another people? What gave them the right—other than military might—to govern this foreign land? Unfortunately, countries are not the only entity that infringe upon the autonomy of others.

When Mom died, communication opened up more between the siblings. The girls understood that they were going to be left the rest of the estate. We knew that Mom made Lorne sign a prenuptial agreement. I never saw a copy of it. We had asked for a copy of it in the legal dispute but were never shown what it said. There was not much left at all. The Bank of Melrose might have still been a part of the estate. A couple of the apartments—Richardson Avenue and the one on West Wyoming Avenue—were still there.

A couple of weeks after Mom died, Lorne called my sister Edithann and told her Mom had left everything to him. She was shocked. The way it was worded, Lorne had to live six months in order to get the estate. But if he died shortly after her, the estate would go to the girls. Edy was the smart one in school and was typically the family mediator. My brother and I were out, though, because of our previous lawsuit. If all the rest had been left to my sisters, certainly my anger would have abated. At least things would have stayed in the family. I was fine with struggling financially personally. I was not fine with the man who led my mother to drink herself to death being the sole inheritor of my father's fortune.

The rest of the girls were in absolute shock. One line in Mom's will said she "intentionally makes no bequest to [Joe, Paul, or the girls] and that she trust[s] that they shall each fully comprehend the reasons for my actions." Because Joe and I had been in previous litigation, we understood fully being left out of the will. But our sisters called us boys to ask for advice. Particularly troubling was that the will Mom wrote in 1993 made provisions for our children, her grandchildren. She had previously left ten thousand dollars each to each living grandchild.

In the midst of all this confusion, we called and hired lawyers. We hired Donald Conn from Peabody, who was actually from Melrose where Dad built his buildings, and the girls hired Hanson Reynolds. We filed an affidavit that argued Lorne had undue influence. Our argument was that he caused her to change her will, to his own benefit, while she was not in her right mind. State of Massachusetts allowed that lawsuit to take place. The first stage was for us all—Joe and my sisters and me—to go through some more depositions and discovery. We struggled to make payments to our lawyers during this process, and we were burned up by the fact that Lorne was using our family's money to defend himself while we were barely scraping by. It later came out that Lorne was still paying arrearages, or late payments essentially, for his child support.

Conn dismissed the case without asking my brother and me. He never brought us into his office to tell us that he was giving it up. He never gave us any warning that he was going to tell the judge that he wanted to drop it for a lack of evidence. But he'd never lost a chance to tell us that he was "going to make mincemeat out of these Boston lawyers." He came to the appeals, later, even though he knew that he had already dismissed us from the case. We were dismissed halfway through the case, and he kept charging us. He played us like fools.

Judge Donnelly gave us a trial date. Lorne Buchanan's lawyers went before an entirely different judge by the name of Bornstein, who dismissed the case on a motion that Judge Donnelly had denied. Lorne's lawyers pushed for dismissal for a lack of evidence, but Donnelly had disagreed with that motion and given the Ventura children a trial date. But Judge Donnelly also left the motion ruled without prejudice and Lorne's lawyers brought up the same motion again in front of a different judge. Bornstein She bought it without so much as an argument. I honestly think the lawyers fixed this case with my own family's money. In other words my belief is that Lorne Buchanan bought this case with Ventura family's money.

Every lawyer I talked to told me that it was highly unusual for someone to dismiss a case like this. This was done at the start when, in the first couple of weeks, they did not see much evidence—not at the end after being given a trial date. That judge didn't know anything about the case, had heard none of our arguments. I have long wondered why that case was dismissed. How could she tell that we didn't have any evidence? It's a wonder how Lorne at this time was able to sell the piece of land Mom was going to give to me in our settlement—and also the family camp, all of which should have been frozen properties. I often wonder what might have happened had he not sold those. Maybe my family would have had our trial.

When they dismissed the case, it absolutely crushed my family. We were shocked that, somehow, the people in this state—who were supposed to be educated and aware of issues of fairness—could hear the story of Lorne Buchanan and not think that he had exerted undue influence over a woman as drunk and out of her right mind as Mom. We appealed. The lawyer didn't want to do it.

Lorne sold our camp before anything was dismissed. He knew what it meant to us kids, and I think he sold it partially to piss us off. He gloated when we ran into him, talking frequently about how good it felt to "win."

He'd pull up beside me in a BMW, looking for me to start trouble.

My brother would say, "Can't you just give the girls something reasonable? You have to take it all?"

"Oh, your mother wanted me to have it," he replied.

When I look back at the rulings of the judge, I am shocked at their rationale. The judge argued that we did not prove the "isolation, health problems and [Mom's] alcoholism unduly influenced her to leave Lorne the estate." They further insisted that our assertions were not "factual" or "provable." But let me tell you what they view as a lack of factual support. The lawyers asked us during our depositions to recall specific instances when we had seen our mother drink too much with Lorne. When we did so, they then asked us what year that was, as if the year had anything in the world to do with anything.

When we struggled to place specific events in specific years, they viewed that somehow as an attack on our claim's credibility. The burden of proof for us was to provide specific facts that (1) an unnatural disposition was made (2) by a person susceptible to undue influence to the advantage of someone (3) who had the opportunity to exercise that influence (4) and that someone in fact used that opportunity to procure the disposition.

What in the world had we not proven out of those four items? What is more valuable proof as to a woman's susceptibility to someone else's influence than the opinions of her children? The ruling of the judge said that excessive alcohol consumption was insufficient to establish Mom's susceptibility to her husband's suggestions. They argued that we couldn't establish without question the status of Mom's ability to think rationally. If a child can't do that about his or her parents, I don't think we have much room in our society for subjective judgment.

BOARD OF BAR OVERSEERS

Years earlier, I had contacted the Massachusetts Board of Bar Overseers about Nelson Lovins not putting a stay on the case. I told them that he didn't show up for court, which seemed to get them interested. In general, they seemed intrigued when I mentioned his shortcomings, but when I brought up the fact that Nelson had tried to get me to sign over my house on collateral, they seemed less surprised. I guess lawyers expect greed from their colleagues.

When I reached the board originally, they'd told me that some-one would be in touch. A week or so later, I received a phone call from someone by the name of Eisenhut. From my perspective, all this guy did was hem and haw. He was difficult, second-guessed everything I said and, in general, didn't seem willing to believe what I was saying. Talking to him was more like debating with an antagonist than talking with an ally. In the end, he did not side with me.

After the investigation, Eisenhut ruled that Nelson's actions had seemed negligent rather than an example of malpractice. To charge your client—legally—a huge sum of money for doing a crappy job seems to me to be, if not technically malpractice, at least immoral. After all, the only way I could fight that particular bill was to hire another lawyer for a civil suit. We've seen how that path worked out for me. Most frustrating to me in a series of actions that led to little was the representatives at the Board of Bar Overseers refusing to allow me to meet with someone in person. We talked only on the phone. I have always been a face-to-face sort of guy, and I wonder if they would have responded to my requests for help with a bit more humanity. They certainly didn't respond to anything over the phone.

Where, in this land overseen by Lady Justice, was the justice that my family so richly deserved? Where was fairness in all of this? And wasn't the old lady, Justice that is, supposed to be blindfolded to symbolize that Justice is indeed blind? If so, why did I feel as if I was running up against a series of allegiances and relationships?

My next interaction with the board was hardly better. After Mom died and the case was dismissed, I started to get a bad feeling about the way that things had happened. The person with whom I spoke only gave me a first name: Luke. After we'd spoken a few times, he told me that he was going to do me a big favor.

"I'm really going to hook you up. This is the best guy. You aren't goanna get anyone better on the board."

"Oh. Thanks!" I responded. I was so excited to have finally reached someone with the power to do something about our plight. When he called a couple of days later, I learned that the gentleman's name was Rosenfeld. I must admit that the first few times I spoke with him, I didn't find Luke's description of him to be accurate. He was gruff and short with me, and he didn't really express any sympathy for my situation. I asked repeatedly to come in and meet face to face. He always gave the same response.

"There's no purpose in doing that," he said. "I have all your paperwork here, and we are very busy down here. This is the most efficient way for me to do things."

After many phone calls and numerous letters with attorney Rosenfeld his response to my letters to the Board addressed to him' was to stamp the letters with a Board of Bar of Overseers stamp and mail them back to my house. I didn't let it drop, though.

I called him back and asked for an explanation of his rationale. In particular, I pressed him on issues that I still considered unresolved. The whole reason I'd called attorney Rosenfeld was to find out whether or not what Donald Conn had done was legal. Dismiss your clients out of a case without their knowledge. Also "Can a case actually be dismissed? After all discoveries have been made and the case has been given a trial date ? Can you show me some case law that covers this?"

To these questions, which I still view today as rational and fair, Rosenfeld responded with little but anger. He wouldn't explain anything to me rationally. He talked to me as if I was beneath him, although I certainly never had any grand respect for his intellect.

After he dismissed the investigation, I wrote letter after letter because he wasn't always available to talk on the phone. When he did answer, Rosenfeld grew angrier and angrier at my persistence.

"Would you just leave me the hell alone?"

"Respectfully, Mr. Rosenfeld, I won't."

Nonetheless, I eventually started to view the Board of Bar Overseers as a dead end with very little to offer me. But I couldn't drop the broader pursuit. I wrote the governor's office. At the time, the Governor is Deval Patrick. I bet if you look up *surprised* in the dictionary, you'll find a picture of my face from when I actually heard from the lieutenant governor, Timothy Murray. At first, we went back and forth on the phone. He was sympathetic.

"I know you are upset, Mr. Ventura. I am sorry that you have been through all of this. But I don't have much authority the only thing I can do for you is to tell you to hire an attorney."

"Ah. With all due respect, sir, I've been through that. I have no money for any more lawyers. They've already eaten through my life's savings."

"I'm sorry. But that is all I can offer," he said.

Who in the government actually had the power to do anything? And why were they running for offices anyway if they couldn't actually help their constituents? The political process, alongside the legal one, continues to grow farther and farther from my realm of comprehension.

Nonetheless, upon his advice, I started to skim the yellow pages. A lawyer I needed? Well, a lawyer I'd hire. I figured if I gave it enough shots, I was bound to stumble across someone who was fair and effective. They can't all be crooked, right? Well, finally, luck was on my side. The first lawyer I came across had an ad that said something about "Family/Probate Legal Counsel," Stoneham, Massachusetts. When I looked at the address listed, I noticed that this place was right down the street. I could have walked. The office was right next to the place where I go for coffee in the afternoon during breaks from work.

I called, and a female attorney told me to come down right away. So I left the three-hundred-unit apartment complex at which I was working in Stoneham and went down to her office. She welcomed me in and listened with a sympathetic face to my plight. After considering it, she responded, "Mr. Ventura, I can help you. But it is going to take some time and effort. And time and effort in the legal world usually equals money. I will need to go to the courthouse and track down some information. Right now, I'll just charge you an eight-hundred-dollar retainer."

When she uttered this figure, I was torn by a couple of different feelings. On one hand, I was excited that I actually had the amount of money that she proposed. But on the other, if I paid her, my account would pretty much be wiped out. And I didn't just have myself to worry about here. I had my son Mateo to care for. I didn't know what I would do without that cash, but I did know for sure that I'd struggle to pay the bills.

But with my personality, and after all these years of pursuing this thing, I felt like someone was finally on my side. So I went after work that morning and dropped off the check at her office.

"Here it is. The money for work to be done. I hope you can do something with it that helps."

"Me, too, Paul. I'll be in touch within two weeks."

It didn't even take her that long. She called me into her office after just a week.

"Paul," she started, "I've done a good bit of digging. Man, have you been through a lot!"

"Yeah."

"You had the thing with that lawyer, Lovins, which, from what I could find seemed fishy to say the least."

"Yep."

"And then I found that you had a settlement agreement with your mom—"

"Yeah, but it was never honored."

"I know that it wasn't in court. But she died not a year after proposing it. You all could have invoked that settlement for twelve months after she died. Your lawyer didn't tell you that when you lost the case?"

"No. What do you mean?"

"Well, in the state of Massachusetts, if someone dies, then their heirs have one year to contest all previous rulings regarding their estates. Someone should have told you that. Your lawyer should have told you that," she said. "And," she continued, "I have some other news for you as well. Something else I don't think you knew."

"What's that?"

"Your lawyer in the case that was protesting the will, what was his name...?" she mused.

"Conn."

"Yeah, he dismissed you from the case at a really weird time."

"He what?"

"He dismissed you and your brother during depositions and discovery, the most important part of the trial. Around the time when you had all paid all the money to have the depositions and discovery done, he dismissed you both from the case."

"I don't understand. I mean, when it came time for him to question Rick Plouffe at the deposition, Conn stood up and left really quickly. He made excuses for what he had to go do. I wondered what he was doing, giving up our opportunity to question their witnesses."

"That never even went to trial. And the judge agreed that you and your brother should be dismissed. So all that money was wasted. And when he was sitting there during those depositions, he was charging you for time that wasn't worth anything. And I've never seen plaintiffs dismissed at that particular time. It seems to me that you had plenty of evidence, but you never got your shot."

I grew red in the face and could feel myself getting more and more livid.

"Are you OK?" she asked. "You look like very pail"

"Yeah. I am just shocked. I can't believe the judge didn't stop him from doing this. Or at least ask for confirmation, through a letter or something, that this was what the client wanted."

In a written summary of her findings, the attorney said that she was "concerned that there seemed to have been a breach by your mother of the agreement which you and she had agreed upon in dismissing the action in the 1987 Superior Court."

She also said, though—and this was the bad news—that I should contact "an attorney specializing in attorney malpractice [to] promptly review for you this matter, and I urge you to do so as soon as possible."

Briefly frustrated to hear one attorney, who'd just taken my last bit of savings, tell me to contact yet another attorney, I told her that I'd be in touch. I went immediately to punch out work for the day at work . I drove home, walked right in the house, and looked through all of my old papers for the number to Donald Conn's office. In perhaps the biggest surprise of the day, I was actually able to get him on the phone. I'd never been able to get him on the phone when he was representing us.

"Hello, Mr. Conn?"

"Yeah, who is this?"

"Paul Ventura."

"Oh, Paul," he said, feigning excitement to speak to me. That excitement quickly turned to dread when I responded to his question, "What can I do for you, Paul?"

"Well, I've been doing some research. And I've found something a bit strange."

"What is that?"

"Why did you dismiss my brother and me from the case without with telling us?"

He paused before answering, with a hint of suspicion in his voice. "Who knows about this?"

I went ballistic. "Who knows about this? What the hell are you talking about? What comment could you possibly have made that would have implied guilt more than what you just said? What did you do to me?"

"Ah…ah, Paul. Calm down."

"Calm down? I want all of our paperwork. Every bit of it."

"Well," he scrambled, "I have to have a written letter documenting that kind of request."

"You'll get it, you SOB."

When I received those documents from Mr. Conn, I found that he had in fact dismissed us. Why he hadn't told us was now suspicious rather than mystifying. This seemed to me criminal. *Who to call to report crimes?* I thought. The DA's office. I called then and asked if I could get a meeting. This was criminal and fraudulent activity. We are talking millions of dollars' worth of motive here. I called the number that I'd saved, and a woman told me that an investigator would call me back. When he did, the guy reminded me of those people with whom I'd worked during the Board of Bar Overseers nonsense. He ignored all the details I gave him, encouraging me instead to file a civil case.

"Civil, huh," I responded with frustration. "What do you have to do to get to criminal court here?"

"Sorry, Mr. Ventura. That is all I can do for you."

OTHER OPTIONS

I got nowhere with the board. I began to feel more and more frustrated with government entities that don't actually do their job. I'm not someone who is overtly political or anything. All I want is for someone who, when they are paid to do something, well...that they do it! Call me old-fashioned in that regard. I don't care if they do it quickly even. I just care that it's done.

That isn't what happened at first with the DA. I expected action from them at least. That is what you see on *Law & Order*. Nobody is ever just sitting around doing nothing. But in my case, they were worthless. And worse than that, they had all my legal documents. I finally pestered them enough to get them to give those back. And what did they use to send them in an Italian meatball box. What a slap in the face why because my dad's family is Italian I just don't understand what they were trying to say. I decided to step it up a bit and go to the next level.

Well, the next level up was the attorney general's office. I wrote them a long letter explaining the problems that I'd faced and my hopes for their efforts at restitution. I had never been someone afraid to express myself via old-fashioned snail mail, and this was no exception. If only all that time spent writing those letters had done some good.

The Commonwealth of Massachusetts
Office of the Attorney General
One Ash burton Place
Boston, MA 02108-1698

I would appreciate you re-evaluating the criminal investigations re: Lorne Robert James Buchanan. The evidence for a re-evaluation will all be found in a deposition of case docket no: 98P532EP. This case was terminated on a renewed motion a week before trial even though the very same motion had already been denied by the court. This meant that the information gleaned in the deposition regarding Lorne Buchanan's guilt was never brought to trial. In these depositions you learned how Mr. Buchanan got my mother Edyth Ventura to change her will while intoxicated on alcohol. Lorne Buchanan knew that if my mother was to continue drinking she would have very little time to live. And yet he continually took her to bars and drinking establishments.

In these depositions Lorne Buchanan admitted to bringing my mother to these establishments and afterwards taking her to her attorney's office to change her will. If in fact these papers or the people who gave these depositions were brought forward I am certain that more facts and evidence would see the light of day.

I believe that if all parties were spoken to it would have grown more and more clear that too many people in this case had criminal intentions.

On March 29th of 2000 I asked this office for a criminal investigation of Lorne Buchanan and was told that, after a careful initial review, this matter had been determined not to fall within certain guidelines. Please respond and let me know if I fall within the guidelines to reopen this criminal investigation. Those who were involved in this tragic abuse of power and injustice must be brought to justice.

Sincerely,

Paul Ventura

Following this letter, the attorney general wrote back to say that they would see me. I told them that I'd been to the DA's office, and that I needed someone with more authority to look into this. An investigator came in and shook my hand. This was the first time that I'd ever been asked to come into a building. He treated me like a human being. He sat there and took notes for a while. He told me that he would get back to me. But he never did.

When Martha Coakley won the election for attorney general in 2007, I wrote her. I wondered if a new face in this office would perhaps give new credence to my concerns. In response, I got a letter that talked about how the "AG's office receives inquiries on a daily basis. Each is reviewed and decisions are made regarding whether or not to investigate further." Essentially it ended with the AG's office: "Will not be further pursuing your complaint." I called and pressed them on the notion that they didn't have the resources. The *Globe* and *Herald* had recently done a big story on some small-potatoes political corruption that involved several thousand dollars. They had the time for that, but not for this?

The woman with whom I had been speaking recommended in a letter that I take this to another agency. "Unfortunately, we will not be able to take any further action on your inquiry or complaint. You have raised one or more issues that generally are not handled by this office, do not fall within this office's jurisdiction, or are more appropriately handled by another agency."

I was frustrated beyond words but hardly willing to stop pursuing my slice of justice. I called and called the AG's office, specifically to ask what agency I should call. But I just kept getting the runaround. I was a bit surprised, however, when the state police called.

"Mr. Ventura?" "Yeah, this is him."

"This is the state police. We are getting reports that you are harassing the attorney general's office."

"Wait! Wait!" I responded with disbelief. "You even know what this is all about? And what this is regarding?"

When the other end of the phone responded, "Why don't you tell me?" I loosened up a bit. At least he seemed receptive. After telling him the Cliffs Notes version, he seemed to come around. He didn't know what they'd meant when they assigned him to be the particular person hassling me. He at least agreed to send back the documentation. He even apologized for all the stuff that I'd been through. I couldn't believe my ears, actually. I do wish that sympathy could have been currency for justice, but I'd rather have one of them than none.

I was defeated. I had almost given up hope for finding out any semblance of truth when I one day saw an advertisement on television: "Has your family been defrauded? Do you have questions?"

At those two lines, boy did my ears prick up. Two questions could hardly have described my plight any more perfectly.

"If you have been defrauded," the ad continued, "call Bill Galvin, secretary of state. He is here to serve the people of Massachusetts to make sure they have a voice." *Well hell*, I thought, *I'll give it shot.* It was a shot that would later impact everything. That same morning, they were greeted by my voice on the other side of the hotline. They talked to me like I was an actual human being. They were nice to me. I thought that I might get some results here. But, when they got back to me, I was due for more frustration.

"Mr. Ventura, this is Bill Galvin's office. We are calling regarding your inquiry and request for investigation."

"Yeah. What do you have for me?"

"Well, we are going to recommend that you talk to the Board of Bar Overseers, as they are the organization that deals with this dimension of the legal system."

"Of course," I said, with more than a little disdain and disappointment in my voice. I don't guess the woman on the other end caught that.

"Why haven't you been there yet?"

"I have," I responded curtly.

"And, what happened?"

"I have already talked to them. I got nowhere," I responded, sure that the disappointment would be audible in my voice this time.

"Who did you talk to?" she asked, as if she would know and offer some subsequent information.

"Well, I talked to this guy named Rosenfeld."

"Huh," she responded, and I thought to myself that the name must not have rung a bell. "Well, you call back and bring down the weight of this office on your request."

"OK," I responded. I felt a ray of hope because I now had a friend in a high place.

I wrote a letter saying that I'd spoken to Bill Galvin's office. They responded to my letter with a phone call, and I spoke with a woman named Anne Kaufman. At first, I had written her a long letter that detailed my story. But, in my anger and frustration, I forgot to list the attorney's name.

She wrote me back and said, "The Office of the Bar Counsel investigates complaints of ethical misconduct against attorneys registered to practice in the Commonwealth of Massachusetts. Our jurisdiction is limited to violations of the Massachusetts rules of Professional Conduct that regulate the practice of law in this state. We are unable to identify the attorney with the information given."

When I got back in touch to clarify what I was looking into, I started by telling her about my previous interactions with Rosenfeld. Imagine my surprise—though I guess I should now be past the point of surprise in this whole mess—when she told me that no one worked at the board by that name. In fact, Rosenfeld hadn't worked there in ten years. He used to be on the board, but now he was an attorney. So why had he responded to me as if he was a member of this oversight organization? Why did he stamp all of my letters with "Board of Bar Overseers" at the bottom?

I went home. I spread the papers all over the floor. It was like something in the movies where the character gets eaten up with this desire to solve a crime. I looked at some of the old legal documents. There must have been a hundred pieces of paper. I looked past the letterhead, but a name caught my eye: *Rosenfeld*. This guy was one of the attorneys on that firm's letterhead.

What the hell? I had a sort of epiphany. That's it! This guy was covering it all up! He was pretending to talk to me as if he cared, but he was actually the opposition.

Not only was he not on the Board Bar of Overseers, but he was also on the other side of the case. This was a cover-up!

Without thinking much about my options, I called the law offices of Rosenfeld. When I was asked who I was and what my call regarded, I gave a fake name and some silly excuse for calling.

Finally, I reached the man and the desk that I was seeking. "Mr. Rosenfeld?" I asked.

"Yeah. With whom am I speaking?" he responded. I couldn't hear lies in his voice, but I knew they were there under the surface.

"Paul Ventura. Do you remember me?"

"Yes."

The pause couldn't have been more than a second or two before I heard a click on the other end.

But now I was sure that something big was happening. But I wouldn't have any of the same luck again with the secretary of state's office. They picked up on the civil court chorus, and my last advocate was lost. I thought that I might be as well.

I called the Middlesex district attorney and sent them the documents, thinking that a more local authority might be interested in this type of fraud. I heard back from them that they had "reviewed the documents [I] sent regarding [my] mother's estate. As we discussed on the phone earlier today, I do not find there is any evidence which would warrant opening a criminal investigation by our office."

Yet another dead end by a do-nothing governmental agency.

But from somewhere within—maybe it was from pleasant memories of mornings in the work truck with Dad—I summoned up the determination to do something more about this.

As a last-ditch effort, I decided to seek help from the FBI. After all, the state hadn't done anything for me, and I seemed to have exhausted all of my options through them. It seemed that, no matter how deeply I dug, I would never reach the bottom of this corruption, nor would I reach someone who would actually do the right—or just—thing. It took me a while to get up the nerve to go to the feds, though. I mean, it isn't the easiest thing to go into the office of those guys you see in action movies. When I finally worked up the nerve to go in, I was sweating bullets, hoping that I could tell my story to the best of my ability.

The one thing that gave me a sense of calm was an episode of sheer luck. Man, I couldn't remember the last time I'd had some of that. As I was driving into the city, I pulled up short at traffic heading into the Big Dig tunnel. The car next to me was driven by a younger lady who would have looked familiar had I been alert enough to notice, but my mind was rehearsing my speech to these federal agents. Thankfully, the other driver was persistent. I saw the passenger side window come down. I had to take a double look. I looked over to the car on my left. Holy smokes! It was Nicole. My daughter.

As I lowered my window, I was struck by that old familiar voice. "Hi, Dad."

"Oh my gosh, Nicole. I haven't seen you in ages," I responded, rubbing my eyes in disbelief. "You look so beautiful." We didn't have enough time to linger and catch up, but as the other drivers behind us started to urge us forward with the more insistent version of honking on their horns, I shouted to her as we pulled away, Please call me when you get a chance.

What a weird coincidence. To be heading in to try to finally achieve some justice for actions in the past, and to have one of my favorite portions of that past pull up beside me. I reached a previously unimaginable calm as I pulled up to the unmarked building.

As I approached the doors, that stress returned. I had wished that Nicole was by my side. As I walked toward the grand glass doors that said "Federal Bureau of Investigation," a younger guy interrupted me.

"Can I help you?"

"Yes, sir," I responded, telling him that I was heading to a meeting with someone and had arranged a time to talk with an agent. He asked for more details, so I gave him the brief spiel, a bit odd that he wanted to talk about this outside of the office in the hallway.

Before I'd gotten too far into my complaints, he interrupted me: "This isn't federal," he said. "This is state. You're in the wrong place, and you need to leave."

I protested timidly, "But—"

"No buts, sir," he responded, as he hustled me out of the building.

I was shaken, but I'd worked up the nerve to show up. I felt that I could summon a bit more nerve to go insist upon being heard once and for all. I went back into the building. I'd seen this guy walk into the cafeteria, so I followed him to track him down. I was sick and tired of the runaround about jurisdiction, whose area it was, and so on. I knew that if I reached the feds, they could trump everything. So I felt a bit of courage as I reentered the building and asked the guy, "Can you show me your badge?"

He did, and he ushered me out once again. I was stronger in my response this time. "But I had an appointment. I thought I'd get to talk to someone in an official capacity. You didn't take notes. And you seem to be in too big a hurry to deal with this anyways. I want to see a supervisor."

"Sir," he responded with anger in his voice, "leave."

I called the F.B.I offices on the way home, hoping to talk to the friendly person who'd encouraged me to come in for a chat in the first place. They didn't seem to be on the same page as this jackass who'd kicked me out without listening to a word I said. In fact, the guy on the phone told me to bring all my documentation and to come back in for an official interview.

The next visit went a bit better. At least I got to talk to someone who listened. But it was far from perfect. When I arrived at the front lobby area of that office, the woman at the front desk directed me to take a seat. I sat and waited for what felt like an eternity. A gentleman came out and tersely took my documents after first patting me down. After about an hour, I was called in to a back room. There was a window between two segments, like we were in jail. I was nervous. And when the agent came to question me, without any sort of greeting or small talk, I was rattled enough so that I probably didn't do the best job that I could have.

As I left the building that day, my heart sank. I didn't think I could go on. I actually turned to the wisest soul that I knew. I told him that I needed a sign. I couldn't go on without some external source of comfort and encouragement. I banged upon my steering wheel as I gathered my wits in the truck. *If you want me to keep going with this, Dad, I need some sort of help. A sign at least. Just give me a sign. Let it snow or something.*

That evening, even though it was a bit early, the first snow of the year arrived. And once it started that year, it felt like every day brought more clouds, more flurries, more whiteouts. The piles of snow that year were unbelievable. It was a record year. I plowed all winter. It didn't stop. In fact, roofs were caving in on buildings. At that point, I told my dad we were good and that I knew he was looking over me, and also that I loved him. Having been granted this sign, I now knew what I had been feeling all along: I needed to push forward. Dad had never been someone to let things stand in his way. Who was I? I was his son. That's who.

Meeting Maria

In the midst of all this turmoil and my efforts to extract from these culprits some dimension of truth and justice, things in my personal life did not grind to a halt. In particular, a relationship developed that would, after some hard moments and tough times, result in the sunlight of my life to this day: my son Mateo.

One of my friends at the car repair place, Performance Plus, decided against my will and with no prodding from my perspective to fix me up on a blind date. He meant well, and I might have thought the same way if I'd been him. I've never been one to go out and prowl for girls on my own, and I certainly wasn't in a place in my life where I would resist a woman's hand around the house. So I went along with it. The mechanic on my end knew a girl named Mary, and the two of them had come to some agreement about fixing up their mutual friend. The friend, Maria, lived in Somerville with Mary. So after some cajoling and encouragement by my mechanic matchmaker, I went to their apartment one Friday night.

They say that the way to a man's heart is through his stomach. I've also heard that "face powder will get a man, but baking powder will keep him." Well, on that evening the cooking drew me in above all else. I was most impressed with how well Maria looked. She was a very good-looking Portuguese girl. The big glasses of wine on the table and the bottle next to it suggested that this would be a fun evening. The festive music in the background made me feel relaxed. Later, in retrospect, I would realize that the prevalence of alcohol in the room should have raised a red flag.

Despite the positive culinary experience, our time together grew more and more awkward as the night wore on. She struck me during this first impression as being painfully shy. I prodded and asked questions about her background. "Where are you from?" and "How long have you lived here?"

These were easy questions. But my attempt at small talk rendered just that: single-word phrases in response that left our conversation just as dead as it had been before. After several stunted attempts to get past this initial level of awkwardness, I got up to leave pretty abruptly. At some point I broke and couldn't endure this severe level of awkwardness. My ability to maintain involvement in the evening declined with the wine buzz. As I ran out the door, eager for the whole experience to be over, Maria's girlfriend, Mary, ran out. She must have been summoned by Maria because she'd been in one of the back rooms to give us some privacy. "Paul," she asked, "where are you going?"

"Oh, I don't know," I responded. "I just don't know that this is going to work, Mary. She isn't saying anything, and I don't know what to do here."

"No, no, no," she reassured me. "She is just nervous. Come back up. She is a great girl. You'll like her. And she told me to come out here to stop you, so I'm pretty sure she likes you."

When I went up, it wasn't as if the conversational floodgates opened up or anything. But Maria did make more of an effort to ask me some questions. And she started to respond to my own inquiries with more than one-word answers. By the end of the evening, as I stood up in a more relaxed manner to make a more timely and gracious exit, we exchanged numbers. This would not be the last time we saw each other.

Things accelerated pretty quickly with Maria, and before either of us knew it, she had moved in. The first couple of months after she moved in were great. I had someone to talk to, and she seemed to sympathize and empathize with my troubles regarding Dad's property. The one thing Maria told me and I think she was right she said it was jealous people that destroyed my dad's real-estate empire and I think she was so right in her thoughts. I also had, on a practical level, someone who could help me keep the house tidy. On the most emotional of levels, though, there was the food. Maria cooked the best meals. She prepared a whole range of traditional Portuguese dishes. I never could get the names exactly right, but there was a variety of seafood. Rice seemed never ending. And on one evening, I was introduced to Chorizo—a spicy sausage that I really liked. In some ways it reminded me of the spicier varieties of Italian sausage. I wasn't used to those types of dishes, but I ate during those weeks until I felt that I might explode. It had been too long since I had a home-cooked meal. I'd never been much of a cook myself, so to have something that someone had labored over and produced the right kinds of flavors...well, this was heaven.

The relationship was not a one-sided affair in which I got all the benefits. She got lots out of this deal as well. I got her a job cleaning condos for work, which meant that she had an income to buy herself stuff that she'd been wanting for years. Together, we had money to make improvements In the basement apartment of my house. She added a woman's touch. She insisted upon curtains and a rug. If I'd provide the money for those things, she had good ideas and would help implement them.

The changes in her, and in my perception of her, were subtle at first. And issues—when we had them—were almost always on Saturdays. She'd go out with some girlfriends and come home a bit tipsy. Later, she stopped coming in on those long evenings at all. Whenever she drank, she'd be more argumentative. But we were always good by the end of the next day. And if we weren't, she begged me for forgiveness and always won it. Then the drinking became more severe. Saturday evenings were compounded by

Friday night benders, and then Sunday became a day of drinking as well. Around year three in the relationship, things grew a bit more severe. They went from distracting and frustrating to all-encompassing and dangerous. Altogether, we dated for about five years.

On one occasion, I received a call from the Lahey Clinic. It seemed that Maria had been in an automobile accident, and they wanted me to come down right away.

"Mr. Ventura. We see from our files that you are Mrs. Rodrigues's contact person. And she asked us to call you during one of her more coherent moments. She has been in a car wreck. She is stable, but the injury to her foot is really severe. We are having a hard time communicating with her and would like for you to come down to the clinic."

Still drowsy from the deep sleep in which they'd caught me, I responded as I rolled out of bed, "I'll be there as quickly as I can."

When I arrived, they took me in to see her. From my uneducated medical perspective, it looked dire. Her foot was gravely injured. Slowly I gleaned the story from her. She'd been out at some party. She drove home drunk in someone else's car, someone who knew that he was too drunk to drive and had talked Maria into driving for him. She foolishly agreed to that plan. She'd gotten her foot sliced up in a portion of the metal undercarriage of the car as it collapsed on impact. Later on, when I saw the car, I found it difficult to understand how this was the extent of her injuries. But in this moment, to make matters worse, Maria was treating the doctors as she so often treated me on those inebriated evenings. She was absolutely belligerent and was now refusing to sign the consent form.

The nurses approached her. "Mrs. Rodrigues, we need you to sign here," to which she responded, "Ahhh" or "Bllaaah" or some other incomprehensible babble. The only thing that was crystal clear in the midst of that nonsense was that she had no intention of touching the pen with which these nurses wanted her to sign. After watching them struggle a bit with Maria, and fully versed and practiced in communicating with this woman, I said, "Let me try."

Walking over to her, I adopted my most firm and clear voice. "Maria. It's me sign the paper if you want to have a foot tomorrow. You are not going to argue with me here. Take this pen and put it on the paper. Then sign."

I physically put the pen in her hand and wrapped her fingers around it. Then, I put the pen to the paper. She scribbled something illegible, but it was good enough for consent.

"Great," said the doctor, who'd been watching impatiently.

Immediately they took her into the operating room, restrained her, and hooked up the sedatives. She was out like a light within five minutes.

As I waited there in the hospital room, looking around at the loved ones who were there for someone else, I began to seriously contemplate calling it quits. This was precisely the kind of nonsense in which Dad had found himself immersed. But I had no kids with this woman. We were not married. What was keeping me tied to this constant source of difficulty? Nonetheless, I knew I couldn't abandon her when she was at this most vulnerable of phases. It was clear that she was going to have limited mobility for the next couple of months. And I knew that Dad—even if he encouraged me to get out of this destructive relationship—would tell me not to leave an injured human being to care for herself. So for the next couple of months, I took care of Maria's every need. I wrapped bandages, changed the gauze, put on the various creams underneath all that, made sure her pills and medications were in order. I continued to dread the weekends because she would drink and we would fight. In addition, she was with another guy in that accident in the first place, a fact that I'd let slide in some ways. But it continued to grate on me.

One night, she decided to tie one on. Around ten or so, I decided that I'd leave her to her own devices. When I rose and told her, "I'm going to bed," she greeted that news with derision. "Sure you are. Sorry I'm not entertaining enough for you."

"It isn't you that doesn't entertain me anymore, Maria. It is you plus the vodka. I know well enough how this night will end, and I don't want to see it. Just stay out of the Jacuzzi, will you?" She'd had a habit recently of going into the Jacuzzi when she'd been drinking, and I knew that was a bad idea.

A couple of hours into my sleep, I suddenly awoke with a sort of weird premonition. As I struggled to clear my mind, a sound registered at the back of it: the motor of the Jacuzzi. The music was still blaring, but I couldn't hear Maria moving around at all. I leaped up from bed and went through the living room in the to the bathroom. There, I witnessed one of the most frightening sights that I've ever seen. There was Maria, floating in the Jacuzzi.

I'm no doctor, but I tried my best to emulate what I'd seen in high school CPR class. I pulled her out of the water and starting pounding on her chest. I pumped her chest once and nothing happened. Quickly again...still nothing. The third time, she wheezed and acted like she was trying to catch her breath. When I realized she wasn't going to drown, but that she also wasn't going to wake up much, I tried to move her to bed. I couldn't budge her. The dead weight was too much. So I rolled her on her side. I went into the bedroom and got some stuff from the bed. I put her head under a pillow, covered her up in a blanket, and went back to bed.

Later that morning, she'd made it, finally, into the bedroom. As she entered, I took that as my cue to get the day started. She struggled to sleep with the sound of banging and knocking, crowbars, and circular saws. She struggled to sleep because, in short, I was tearing that Jacuzzi to shreds. I'd never relax again with it in there, and I probably never should have had it working in the first place. If I couldn't stop Maria from drinking, at least I could take away one possible source of danger to her when she did.

At some point, the drinking got to be too much for me. During the week, she was great. But on the weekends, she'd turn into a monster. And eventually I stopped seeing anything but monster in her. She'd drink and drink. The connection to my memories of Mom were probably the final straw. I began to realize that, once again in my life, my daily routine was being dictated to me by the abuses and addictions of someone else. In fact, I started thinking this is precisely what my father went through. Maria was belligerent more regularly than Mom, though. She broke things, and I'd have to call the cops. I needed no more of them in my life. Finally, I worked up the nerve to end it.

Weeks later—and, by the way, I'd just been on an initial date with another woman—I heard again from Maria.

"Paul," I heard her voice on the phone. "I hope you are doing OK."

"I'm fine," I responded, happy that our relationship hadn't soured too much during the breakup.

"I have some news for you, and I think maybe you'd better sit down."

"What is it?" I asked a bit reluctantly.

"I'm pregnant."

In a nutshell, this was not the news I wanted to hear. I was already having a hard enough time dealing with Kim's attorney over child support. I hardly wanted to compound and complicate my financial situation with another obligation to another woman with whom I had already ended my relationship. Still, here I was.

I wasn't sure the child was actually mine, and I wondered if perhaps this wasn't a ruse to get some money out of me for booze. I pleaded with Maria to get a paternity test, but there really isn't any good way to have that conversation. The implication of my request, of course, is that she'd been sleeping around with a bunch of people. Few women welcome that sort of insinuation. But, I finally talked her into taking the test. I had to agree to pay her rent for a couple of months, but that price seemed well worth it to me for peace of mind and surety. Just one problem: she couldn't take any sort of test until she actually had the baby. So I'd have to wait another few months to find out the answer to this mystery.

One morning months later, Maria called me to tell me that the hospital was telling her they needed to operate to remove the baby. They were worried about some health problems, and they needed to operate that day. She'd just gone in for a regular checkup and had been greeted with this particular news. She had freaked out and left to call me. She was most worried about getting the logistics settled and about the bills that would pile up as see went through this process. In my conversation with her, to keep her calm, I told her not to worry, that I would pay her car payment.

Nonetheless, I was reluctant about going in to the actual birthing process. That night, when her brother called me to tell me that it was time and she was ready to deliver the baby, I still didn't know—at the time—if the baby was mine. But Maria's brother seemed sure enough of it. He called and called, pressuring me. "You need to man up and do the right thing.

I didn't know how to avoid this topic with her brother, or to say without saying that I wasn't sure if I was the right man. Still his calls got my mind spinning. And I knew that if I didn't go in, I would regret it. So I went in. It was really late, around midnight on December 11, 2004, and when I got there I went straight to the nursery. I started looking through the window and saw one of the nurses rolling this tiny creature across in an incubator. He was around eight weeks early and had come by C-section.

The nurses greeted me. In a conversation with the nurses I asked if the child was from my girlfriend Maria they then said yes and asked me if I'm the father and they both started to laugh they let me look only for a few seconds but then I knew this baby is mine. When it came time to sign the birth certificate I wasn't sure if I should.

The nurse paused and looked at me knowingly, as if she'd heard this kind of thing before. "Well, let me tell you, it is a whole lot easier to get the name taken off than it is to get the name put on."

"Huh. I didn't know that."

"What is your gut telling you?"

"Well," I responded, "I think he sort of looks like me."

"Well, then, take the risk and put your name on the birth certificate."

Later that morning, after the sun had risen, her brother Eddie came into the hospital. I was excited to see him and to share the news that Mateo was healthy. He laughed after I'd gotten through excitedly telling him all the news.

"That's great, Paul. I'm happy. But your truck is running outside I couldn't believe I left my truck running for hours.

I went outside and turned off the truck, amazed at how zoned out I must have been to have done this.

Sure enough, the results came back a couple of weeks later for the paternity test. The results pointed their medical fingers straight toward one person: me.

I wanted to rekindle the relationship for the sake of the child. We had some short conversations about it, but it was something that was clearly not happening from her end. I rectified myself to the fact that we'd be a split set of parents.

With his birth, I began to think more and more about the future. Instead of just focusing on the negatives of life, and on the previous injustices that had been committed against my father's name, and against my honor, Mateo's birth ushered me into a new present. I had something new to live for. They'd taken my kids. My wife. My truck. My tools. My connection to family. And for years, all I'd been able to think about were the things that I had lost. When I went into the lawyer's office and made a trust for the family house in Mateo's name, it represented the new start that I was pursuing as well as a new chapter in my life.

CUSTODY OF MATEO

At first, Mateo lived with Maria. We had a pretty good relationship about who would get to see him when, but certainly Maria used Mateo as leverage to get me to buy stuff for her. For example— and this is just one of many—she didn't have a refrigerator in her place. So she complained pretty frequently to me and told me that neither she nor "your son" has a fridge to store food. "How are we supposed to eat healthy, Paul? How am I supposed to get him what he needs to grow up big and strong?"

On other matters, I was less susceptible to this sort of manipulation, but on this front I pretty much agreed with her. Any home with a young child in it had to have a fridge. Plus, I knew where to get quality stuff for discounted prices. I got her a nice Whirlpool fridge, and she was plenty grateful. But Maria's need for money inevitably grew more complicated than initially anticipated. So when I went in to see Mateo again and ended up in that apartment, I noted that she had a much lower-quality fridge. She'd traded or something. To compound my concern, she lived in a trucker's route. All you could smell when you got out of your car to go inside was diesel fuel. I worried about the health and well-being of the child.

I went to the courthouse soon thereafter. I went to the courts because Maria was living in an absolute shithole apartment in Everett. I mean, I wouldn't have wished that place on my worst enemy. Well, maybe I would wish it on Lorne, but on no one else! Worried about my son, I filed the paperwork for visitation and child support.

The first couple of times I went to court, she didn't show up. When she finally did, she was pretty argumentative with the judge. So he turned to me and asked, without my prompting this question, if I wanted to change the paperwork.

"You're going to change these documents, right, Mr. Ventura?"

I was just trying to stay out of the tense conversation that he'd been having with Maria, and I didn't know what he was talking about. "Excuse me?" I asked.

"You want custody, too, not just visitation rights. Correct?"

This question was certainly leading. I responded, not wishing to provoke him, with, "Yes, your Honor."

He then turned and started asking Maria questions to determine what kind of living situation Mateo was in. "Where is your son now?"

She wouldn't tell him. I knew Maria wasn't totally crazy, and that Mateo was probably with someone relatively competent, but the judge didn't know that. He didn't seem used to being stonewalled, and he grew angrier and angrier with her. Finally, as the judge reached a point at which I thought his gavel was going to be thrown, Maria melted and told the judge where Mateo was. Once the judge had that piece of information, he didn't want to go any further until he'd fully investigated it. So he told me to go to the Somerville police station. He wanted me to accompany them to this apartment, to bring Mateo back, and to bring him back with me. Only one problem: when I went with the police, no one was in the apartment. Or at least no one would answer. We knocked and knocked, but to no avail.

The police were ready to give up, but I had an inclination about what was happening. Some of Maria's friends and peers were not documented immigrants. They were uneasy answering the door to anyone who looked official, and what looked more governmental and scary than a couple of burly policemen? Knowing that someone was probably inside, I went around back and tried opening the windows. I found one right near the door that was open. Lucky! I reached my arm inside, unlocked the door, and cautiously entered.

"Hello? Is anyone here?"

No one answered. But when I rounded the corner, I saw a petite woman. I asked her, "Baby?"

She didn't seem to speak English, but she understood me well enough to point toward a bedroom. Upon entering, I saw Mateo lying on the bed. I gathered him up, grabbed his bottles and diaper bag, and headed for the door. The police were surprised to see me exit the door upon which they'd been fruitlessly knocking, but they didn't give me a hard time. When I got back to the courthouse, I was directed to a back room, inside which were two women who worked with the probate court.

The women said that they would take the baby so I could go into the courtroom to report on the state of Mateo. But Mateo wouldn't let go of my neck. I was worried that this might seem somehow a sign that he was scared child, and that thus it would reflect on my parenting. But the women viewed this as hilarious. They had never seen a tiny little baby with such a death grip and strong will. It seemed that they liked what his grip said about my fathering. On the other hand, they were really reluctant to let me go into the courtroom because they figured that Maria would go nuts if she saw me with the kid. In all the delays, Maria finally picked up on something fishy. In response to the judge's refusal to explain to her what was going on, she stormed out of the courthouse. Immediately thereafter, the judge gave me custody of Mateo. I was ecstatic. I knew that this was the best thing for him.

My paternal affections and excitement over getting to care for this little one didn't change one dramatic truth: it wasn't easy to care for an eighteen-month-old baby. Easy or cheap. For one, there were the diapers to change. There was the diet and food to manage. Bottles to shake and warm. I had to switch jobs because with my towing gig the hours were too erratic. I knew that I couldn't leave the house in the middle of the evening with a young child at home. And I also knew that leaving the house in the middle of the night—in short, responding to whatever tow was ordered whenever you could—was the only way to make ends meet in that business. I needed another job.

I'd worked a hodgepodge of jobs in the previous years. As I mentioned before, I'd driven a dump truck for a while. Those coworkers with whom I'd signed on doubted I could hack it at that career, but I showed them! On one particular occasion, I was told to go to Trinity Church next to the Hancock building in Boston. When I showed up, the foreman told me the last two drivers went home because they didn't do four loads to Randolph, Massachusetts. The trucks would back under a conveyor belt to get loaded. Let me tell you, I didn't go home. I couldn't afford to go home. I drove on the highway with one thing on my mind: four loads. When I asked the foreman at two o'clock if he wanted me to run another load, he yelled at me and said, "What are you, an asshole? How many loads have you done?"

"Four."

At first he didn't believe me, but when I told him the guy at the farm told me to slow down, that I was scaring the farm animals driving too fast, he just shook his head and said, "See you tomorrow."

Back at the shop, my boss quipped, "Guess you didn't get to stay on the job."

"Yes, I did."

"Then why are you back so early?" he asked.

"I did four loads, and the foreman said 'see you tomorrow.'"

At any rate, the tow truck gig had been my most regular. Even at that, I probably wasn't hard enough to make a huge living at it. Think about the types of people a tow truck driver interacts with. They are almost all mad at you for towing their car. Many times, they hadn't made the smartest decision in parking in that one spot, so they were hurried or didn't pay attention or just plain didn't like authority. When you are towing someone with car trouble, they tend to be the poor and downtrodden, people whose cars always broke down on them. Rarely do the rich and well-to-do get towed for those reasons. But, every now and then, I'd run into someone who stirred my capacity for empathy.

One evening, I answered a call from a woman stuck on the highway in Concord. When I arrived, I found a younger woman—who looked like a young girl to me—with two young kids. I towed her all the way from Concord to Chelsea. When we arrived, the girl looked at me and asked, "How much do I owe you?" I needed to charge her a bit over a hundred dollars to make money, but I felt bad from the get-go to charge her anything. I looked at those young kids and thought of my own young ones. I remembered all the occasions that I had struggled to make ends meet, and how that affected me as a father. As she started to finger through the last few bills in her wallet, I saw a trace of reluctance on her face. She wasn't going to protest, but I could tell that she could hardly afford it. So I told her not to worry about it. "Why don't you just keep the money this one time, on the house?"

"No, I couldn't possibly."

"Please. This one is on me."

But I knew that if I didn't make money, I couldn't pay my bills; however, on occasion, charity made me feel like a true man.

On another call, a tractor-trailer was broken down on the off-ramp of the highway. When I got there, the driver kept telling me that his truck had to be in New York by two o'clock, or he was in big trouble. At this time of the year, it was so cold I figured the fuel had frozen—and I was right. The driver and I tried for hours to get the truck started. We even put new fuel in the tanks and jumped it off the tow truck, but had no luck. His boss had even called another truck repair company to try, and that guy had no luck. But I wouldn't give up easily.

"How much air pressure do you have in the truck?" I asked the driver.

He knew what I was thinking: we could pull the truck with mine to start it .He said I don't think your truck can pull my fully loaded rig. Let's give it a try I said we have nothing to lose.

It worked, and he gave me a wad of cash. A week or so later, his boss called to thank me. He told me I had saved a huge account for his company and that he would recommend my company to all

he knew. It was one of the best phone calls I'd ever received. I wonder if the gentlemen knew the towing company Ventura Towing
consisted of one man and one old 1988 GMC 3500 tow truck that's
what pulled his fully loaded tractor trailer. I guess you would have
had to be there to see what aim talking about.

So after getting custody of Mateo, I started to think about alter-
natives. Because I knew that this would not work with the baby boy
I now had in my care, I looked for different work for a while but
with no luck. Eventually, though, I saw an ad for a position in property maintenance in the local paper. It looked like something I was
immensely qualified for. So I went in, interviewed, and rocked it.
But then, a couple of weeks after I got that job, the owner of the
business there came to me. "Paul, we pulled your CORI."

"OK. What is that?"

"Well, it's your criminal records."

OK, but I was found not guilty of all the accusations against me, I
thought.

He continued, "In pulling those records, we found documentation of all your difficulties with the ex-wife."

So they had found out about Kim, about all my legal past. I
can imagine how that all looked to him. After all, he didn't know
me from Adam, and he was probably reluctant to get into business
with someone he couldn't trust or count on. I know this because
he later told me that he thought about letting me go right after I
started the job. My saving grace was that old, hardened parole officer. Without breaking his protocol, which stipulates that he can't
say too much about his parolees, he somehow subtly convinced
this owner that I was going to be just fine. He thought that I was a
good person who needed another shot. To this day, I remain grateful for that. People who help other people out—they are too rare
in this world.

These legal troubles continued to plague me, though. About
two months into receiving my paychecks, I found out that Kim's
lawyer had reached me even here. They started garnishing my
wages, taking my child support payments—at the new job—out
of my check. This didn't faze me much. I had no intention of
skipping out on those payments anyway. This just left one less

thing for me to fool with. So for the first six weeks, the job was great. And I presumed that Kim was happy because I was hearing nothing from her. But at the six-week mark, I received a letter from Kim's attorney. Apparently she hadn't seen the first dollar from those payments. She counted on that $150 a week, too, but she had been advised to let me default on my obligation so she'd have a bigger legal case against me. But the problem was, I had been paying!

I was eager to make my court date—I'd received a notice in the mail that I was in contempt for failure to pay child support. I couldn't wait to show them my pay stubs where the money had been taken out of my checks. I had irrefutable evidence this time! No one could call this my fault! Right?

On the documents that summoned me to court, I noticed that this was the same judge that had presided over the case that had been dismissed, Judge Donnelly. When I got to the courthouse, my ex-wife's attorney appraised the situation pretty quickly. Apparently he'd seen it before.

"OK," he said, "this is what you are going to do, Paul. I want you to go over to the offices of the Department of Revenue. This is an issue with their network, and they'll be able to resolve it. I want to get this dealt with today.

Well, as we were walking towards the other court house down the street Mateo's mom, Maria, was walking with him holding his hands. We'd started to spend some more time together, especially on those days when she was sober. But on this day, things just weren't lucky for any of us. Walking on the sidewalk, we stepped onto a crosswalk when she slipped on a granite portion that bordered the brick crosswalk. In the process, she cut her ankle pretty severely and took Mateo down with her, who landed on his head. Immediately a huge bump started to show, and he descended into a full-fledged fit. I couldn't blame him. I knew it must have hurt!

So I went back to the court, carrying Mateo with me. I went in to tell them what had happened. The court officer told me to go get help for my son. He promised that he'd get word to the judge and attorney about what had happened. Wouldn't you know it? The next day, I received a letter that cited me for contempt of court for leaving the courthouse that day. It also charged that I owed $1,200 for Kim's lawyer's time, as he had stayed around the courthouse all day long. Apparently, the court officer hadn't told the judge what had happened, and Kim's lawyer just told the judge that I had left. So now I had a new set of court obligations. Same story, different day. Right?

When I entered the courtroom that next time and explained what had happened, I couldn't believe my ears. Of all the judges' verdicts that I'd been on the wrong side of, this was perhaps the most ridiculous. Judge Donnelly allowed the attorney's fees $1,200 for the attorney staying at the court the whole day. I didn't even owe money for child support in the first place! The only reason I'd been brought to trial at first was that this governmental entity hadn't done its job! They take the payments out of my check and then I get this extra fee. When I went in to protest this fee, Judge Donnelly just looked past the humanity in my face and told me that if I failed to make the payments, I'd go to jail.

The good news is that the relationship between Maria and me eventually began to improve. I think that, deep down, she figured that I would be best for Mateo. She had boyfriends who were bad for her destructive behaviors. I struggled to figure out what to do with Mateo for a while. Some women helped me with him, but eventually those relationships fizzled as well.

Eventually—and this is where the story gets really positive—we ended up at a school called Children's Gathering. This place was a godsend. I was worried after a great interview process that they weren't going to have room for Mateo. This concern was fostered by comments from the woman at the school who'd expressed some reluctance about whether they had space. But they did an interview process with Mateo and brought him in for a day. He was glowing at the end of the day, and the people at the school had no reservations about accepting him after they'd spent a full day with him.

I earned the good graces of the school for doing some work with the woman who ran the school. I fixed some of their drainage issues with a Bobcat and a dump truck, and she continually focused on how much that helped them. I stressed to her that we had helped each other, and that this is the way friendships are supposed to work. I could rebuild the whole school and wouldn't come close what all the teachers did for my son in the three years he was their.

In general, life with Mateo has been an absolute joy. We may never know why the things that happen in life to us happen. And my road to the second round of fatherhood certainly couldn't have been visible to me back on that evening that I met Maria. In fact, she wasn't visible herself on that evening. I thought she was a shy girl, one I would struggle to talk to.

Yet, I have a soft spot in my heart for Maria. She had, after a while, cleaned herself up a bit. At least I didn't have to see her when she is off the reservation and drunk. But she also gave me my heart. I struggled to adjust at first to all the new demands on my time. I had to redirect my work patterns to accommodate the life of a single parent. But every time this kid smiles at me, it all feels more than worth it.

My Saturdays now are all spoken for. We wake up and hang out together. I can't wait for the day when he will be able to work with me teaching Mateo the things that my father taught me in life. People can't take away your ability to work with your own two hands for your living. They can't take away the knowledge and know-how to fix things the way my father taught me. But more than that, they can't take away your refusal to quit on a job like all the people in lawinforcment have done to the Ventura family's hope of receiving any kind of justice. If I can impart those lessons to Mateo, I'll know that my time with Maria was truly a blessing. It will mean that I've been a really good father and have prepared my boy to grow up right.

MOTIVATIONS

I didn't really want to write this book. But I felt like I had no choice after the courts and law enforcement failed to enforce justice. I don't like telling people about my life. But if I don't, that means Lorne and all the lawyers and bankers got away with millions of dollars in stolen real estate. If I don't speak out, that means that my humanity is somehow lost.

I read somewhere about this thing called the Truth and Reconciliation Commission in South Africa. It seems that Nelson Mandela, after years of serving jail time and suffering under the unfair racial policies of apartheid, thought the most important thing was for victims to be able to speak out to those who had harmed them. Witnesses who were identified as victims of gross human rights violations were invited to give statements about their experiences, and some were selected for public hearings. Perpetrators of violence could also give testimony and request amnesty from both civil and criminal prosecution. Here you had victims telling their stories to the people who had harmed them, and later, on camera for video that was broadcast worldwide.

The idea behind this, it seems to me, is to give victims a voice. One of the worst things that happens to victims, especially when they are confronted with a government that has refused to help them in a time of need or has treated them like less of a person than they are, is that they lose faith in the world's ability to recognize them and give them a fair playing field. We base our lives on, and learn in school from an early age about, notions of equality and human rights. When things happen in the world that undermine what we expect in regard to those ideas of fairness, what are our options? One is to lash out with violence and rage. But Gandhi argued that anger actually hurts the person who was angry more than anyone else. By speaking up, by demanding to be heard, we do a couple of things.

We reassert our own humanity through speaking. And when we get others to listen, that assertion is even more powerfully validated. We demand with the very act of speaking, or in my case writing, to be recognized: I am a person! With a voice! I have a story that is uniquely my own. And your story has impacted mine, so you had best listen. By shaping the story, by telling how it happened to me or about how it felt while it was happening, perhaps we set the stage for a better future.

And so my story is a necessary one. I felt as if no justice was granted to me from the system. As a taxpaying member of this society, I was granted civil rights. I was repeatedly and systematically denied the rights granted to me in the constitution. And so I write this book. This is my voice. These pages contain my best attempt at my full self. I wanted to tell the people what they did to my life. Through the very act of telling my story, I wanted to insist that they didn't get away with it, and that I haven't let it rest simply because the courts didn't do their jobs. There may be no further consequence for them, but this is my metaphorical mountaintop, and I'm shouting for all to hear. Those people involved know what they did to my life. Perhaps they haven't thought about it, but I wanted to be crystal clear: in harming me, they also harmed my kids. They harmed my ex-wife and my marriage. My father. My brother, sisters, and mother. Not one person I loved and cared for was spared from the negatives of this experience.

This was my attempt to show what their actions—or inaction—did to the Ventura family. Let the people of the Commonwealth see what the authorities and legal counselors and everybody involved did and didn't do. These were people who were hired or elected to represent their constituents' best interests. And in my case, they failed time and again. Even worse, often they seemed unwilling even to try to help, preferring instead to hide behind the convenient ease of governmental and bureaucratic red tape. So let those people now, after reading this book, render their own judgment on what was right and just and fair.

I believe, and have believed for some time, that the reason that I went to the end of the world to get the truth was because of how close I was with my dad. He was my world, and my motivation throughout these years has been him. He was a father and friend to me. He taught me how to work and how to live life according to a higher good. He taught me how to do the right thing. He taught me to stand up for myself in the face of injustice. He taught me to insist upon my right to be recognized but to do good work when recognized. He made me who I am today, and he somehow instilled in me the strength to dig deeper and deeper into a reservoir of strength I never knew I had.

Compared with my constancy, there were others who followed a different path. My older brothers and sisters gave up. I don't understand how or why they did. They were older than I. They should have been even more upset than I was, having had a longer time in life to cultivate and develop a relationship with Dad; they should have been even angrier to see all that he'd worked for trampled upon. I have not let my mystification with the inaction of my siblings stop me or slow me down. I would have liked some help investigating all the wrongs done to our family, but when help didn't come, I went at it alone. How they just walked away from what was ours I'll never understand. In the case of my other siblings, my younger sisters, I am more understanding. They were too young to fight, and perhaps too young to deal with the reality of what they had been dealt.

I love them all. I help them as much as I can. I would drop anything that I was doing to help them in a time of need. But their attempts to "help" me have been misguided and have underestimated my level of anger and ability to fight for what I know is right. They'd been telling me for years to "let it go" and "let it go." I've thought often of their words. They are, after all, my family, and I know that I've been wrong about some things in my life. But not about this. When do we stand up for what we know is right? Letting something go is a sign of either defeat or concession, and I'm not ready to admit defeat. I may have lost money in this process, but I insist that what happened is wrong. I believe that if I'd had some help in this process, and if the set of fists pounding on those governmental doors had been joined by three other sets— that is, if we'd had been four rather than one—things might have been different. We might have gotten farther.

I don't blame them. They just don't have as much fire in their belly about all this. In short, they aren't as angry as I am. I don't have to summon anger; it just lingers in me as I lay in bed thinking about life. I don't want to be as mad as I am, but what are we supposed to do in the face of this sort of injustice? I swallowed so much shit from the greedy people of this world. I watched Lorne Buchanan pouring vodka down the throat of my mom and then had to deal with his stealing our family's inheritance through killing her. I watched lawyers clamber for money rather than justice. I watched them and dealt with them as they tried to maximize on hours so that they could be paid far too much for their ineffectual time. Who can blame me for not being able to stomach that level of greed and injustice? The world is indeed a fallen place, but that doesn't mean we have to accept it.

I must have ended up with a bit more Italian in me. But the Italian was valuable only in the connection it gave me to my father's spirit. I've done this all for him. And I was able to do it *because* of him.

REGRETS

I'm not proud of all my actions. But I firmly believe that the inaction of good people led to many of my actions.

My sister's boyfriend, Ralph, worked with me over the summers. Dad would give us jobs to do, and he served as sort of an apprentice. He got to make some spending money, and he was a big help. After spending so much time with me, eventually he started to see more and more of my sister Susie.

Their son, Joey, started calling me more and more. One night I finally resolved to call him back. His dad, Ralph, answered and explained that Joey had been having a rough time. Ralph seemed at a loss about what to do with his son. I was pissed at him because Ralph had strong-armed Joey away from Susie in the first place. Now that he had the kid, here he was failing as a father. Susie wanted to clean up Joey, to send him to rehab, and so on. Of course Joey had chosen his father, as that was the path of least resistance. I knew two things: Ralph was too weak to do the right thing, and he would regret the consequences to come from that weakness.

The rumors were rampant and crazy. My sister Marianne told me that he was somehow plugged into the cops, doing buys for them undercover. The other siblings resolved to do something. Susie put him into a program called CHINS, and Ralph took him out of the program. I'm sure he was responding to the pleas of his kid, but sometimes parents need to give tough love if they are going to give love at all.

Ralph was—according to rumors—even doing drugs with his kid. This, after someone living in their house with them had died from an overdose. It grew more and more clear that Ralph was a big part of the problem, not just someone enabling the problem.

I responded to Ralph with strong words of encouragement. Joey was reaching out and looking for help. I'd seen him on the Fourth of July and could tell that he was hooked on some bad drugs. He was probably around eighteen. He'd just finished high school, and he wasn't sure about his direction. But on June 15, 2011, he died at the age of twenty-two.

No one would say exactly what happened. I was at the wake trying to get information from people about what went down. Everyone I asked acted as if they knew nothing. In the funeral parlor, I broke down. I knew that I'd given Ralph good advice about the way to proceed, but I didn't pursue Joey himself, guide him through a rehabilitation process, and make sure that he had a friend during the times that he needed one most. That will continue to haunt me.

Another set of regrets concerns a neighbor who was always good to me. Mr. Forgione lived across the street from my house. He'd known Dad and Mom back when times were better for all parties. He'd been especially close friends with Dad. They took care of each other. Mr. Forgione owned a little store in Malden—a little deli/grocery store that had a liquor store built adjacent to it. Any time one of the mechanical elements of his deli stopped working, he knew who to call: Dad. Even if we had a full morning, Dad always figured out a way to swing by to tinker with whatever wasn't working well. And by the time we left, things were always fixed. In return for these neighborly acts, Mr. Forgione would always make sure we had some special groceries at home. He'd drop off some deli meats, or he would get us a pan of whatever casserole he happened to be working on.

After Dad died, during all of my legal trouble, Mr. Forgione took time and energy to check in with me. He'd bring me meals in the evenings, usually some sort of pasta. He was a great cook, and I reaped the rewards for his skills in the kitchen. He made his own sausages, sauces, and so on. When he made dinner for himself and his wife, he'd make a little extra for me. Everyone else, even my siblings, had given up on me throughout the years. He alone always made sure I had food to eat. He made sure that I had a vehicle when I couldn't get to work.

In return, if he ever had odd projects for which he needed a young set of hands and strong back, I was there for him. I'd fix his appliances if they broke, do odd plumbing stuff for him, and help him with any minor tasks.

His daughter and wife were trying to get him to refinance the house. The daughter wanted to add a little in-law apartment in her basement, similar to what I had, to get some extra income. She wanted her dad to take out another mortgage so that she could have the money from the loan to fix up her place. By this time, Mr. Forgione was retired, and he didn't want to give out the money. Tired of the conversations and saying no again and again, Joe—I always called him Joe or Pasta, for his cooking skills—asked me if he could join me for a couple of days at work. His daughter would come to see him every day rehashing the same old pleas: "Dad, help me out. Dad, give me the money." Instead of dealing with that again and again, finally he decided to dodge the encounter. He'd rather sit in the truck while I did Bobcat work. I enjoyed those days with him, as I had always been open to company.

He joined me for three days in a row. We commiserated about our family problems together, and we would hang out in the garage in the evenings. I'd have a beer; he'd have a tonic; and I'd pick his brain about his experiences. On the third evening of our new routine, he asked me, "Paul, do you mind if I come along again tomorrow?"

"Of course I don't mind, Joe. You are always free to join me, man."

"You sure? I don't want to overstay my welcome."

"I'm positive. If anyone understands family that is getting all over your nerves, it is me."

That next morning, before I was scheduled to pick up Joe, a woman called me and pressured me to hurry over to her house to look at a landscaping project. She wouldn't take no for an answer, and she insisted that I get there as quickly as possible. I figured it was a bit early to knock on Joe's door, so I thought that I'd go look at this project, make a bid, and get back in time to pick up Joe. Turns out, the woman who had been so insistent had absolutely no clue about what she wanted to have done in the yard. I found this out soon after I arrived, as we walked around the yard. She was noncommittal on any sort of decision. Usually, people tell me that they want those bushes out, or that plant moved. She couldn't tell me much of anything about what she envisioned. Frustrated, I told her to get back to me once she was better prepared to make a final decision.

Then I went back to get Mr. Forgione. But when I pulled up to the house, there were three cruisers in front of it. I went to the door and saw one of our neighbors coming out. When I was stopped as I approached the door to the house, I asked the cops, "What is going on here?"

"Well, we believe someone has committed suicide, sir. Stay back."

"What ?"

"The owner of the house shot himself."

"WHAT? Joe!"

I was absolutely beside myself. Here was this guy who had treated me so well. He was perhaps one of my dearest friends. I was shocked. As well as I'd grown to know him, I had not felt that he was depressed enough to take his own life. The Wakefield Police Department never questioned me about his state of mind. How were they going to determine whether or not he was suicide or a crime without talking to the person who'd spent the last three days with him? And why weren't there any state troopers there? Anyone in a suit who looked capable of actually evaluating a crime scene?

Just a couple of weeks after the death, the daughter put the house up for sale. I started to view the situation as a bit more fishy. The more and more I thought of it, the more sure I was.

Mr. Forgione just hadn't struck me as suicidal. He'd been talking so much about how he loved his grandchildren. He had plans to take care of them in his will.

I called the DAs and told them what I'd been thinking. The woman I talked to at the MIDDLESEX DA'S office listened to me with only mild interest and promised that someone would look into it. *Sure*, I thought. *I know what that means.*

One of my regrets, though, is not being a bit more persistent when it came to encouraging lawinforcment to look at the case with a bit more suspicion. I know that police don't want to add to their murder rate, and so they are often all-too-eager to rule something a suicide if that is what it looks like. But I feel like maybe Mr. Forgione would have delved a bit deeper for me if our roles were reversed.

Another occasion that has caused me years of doubts and regrets resulted in more than one death. I was in the oil truck one evening, driving home after being called to deliver oil to a customer that had run out. On my way home from the delivery close to where I park the oil truck something caught my eye when I passed an office buildings.

I looked over to the left and saw a long-haired guy who looked rather questionable. Something about the way he was looking around and pausing before he went into the building led me to believe he didn't want to be noticed. He was carrying a large duffle bag, I couldn't tell if it was empty or full. I wondered if he was going in to rob that office building. You know how you just sometimes have funny feelings about something? Well, my radar for that kind of stuff was going absolutely haywire.

As I pulled the truck over and sat in the truck next to the parking lot of the 7-Eleven I noticed him and had watched him from the truck mirror on the driver's door from the opposite side of the road—I watched as he went in the building it was then I started to dial the cops number on the cell phone and then, spurned and burned by my many interactions with the police, I decided against it. I worried that they wouldn't believe me and couldn't take a chance that there would be another hard time. My justification? He was just stealing stuff, and there really wasn't a whole lot to be done about it anyway. I further excused my inaction by arguing to myself that, if I was wrong about his being suspicious, I would just end up in yet another bout of trouble with the cops.

I didn't know what the building was at the time. Later, I would find out that he worked at an Internet company called Edgewater. I would also later come to regret doing nothing on that evening perhaps as much as I regretted anything in my life.

The next day, the news began to cover a story—still a bit vague on details—of a shooting in Wakefield. Of course, I followed the story with some interest. But when they gave the address, I started to think about the fact that the building was on my drive home. The more I began to think about it, and once I heard a cross street referenced that helped me narrow down the geography, I had a sudden epiphany. That was the same building that I'd seen the guy going into the night before.

When I finally saw his mug shot, which was quickly the topic of every conversation in Massachusetts, I knew immediately the magnitude of my mistake. This hadn't been a robber. It had been a man crazy with rage about a work problem. The news coverage during the weeks and months that followed depicted a guy whose methods and reasoning were mysterious. One article talked about his conviction after failing to convince the jury: I never talked about this for a long time I felt I let all the people that died down so bad. I hope people believe what I'm saying is true. Why I ask God why me to be put through this I cried so many times .I sometimes think I should have kept quiet about this but I needed to set myself free of this painful event in my Life. I wish I had driven the oil truck a different way home or had called the cops like I started to then got to nervous to call.

A man who shot to death seven co-workers at a software company was convicted of murder today after failing to convince a jury that he was so delusional he thought he was killing Hitler and his henchmen to prevent the Holocaust.

The defendant, Michael McDermott, 43, stood impassively as he heard the verdict in a courtroom full of relatives of the victims. The convictions on seven counts of first-degree murder mean Mr. McDermott will be sentenced to life in prison without the possibility of parole. Massachusetts does not have a death penalty.

The jury deliberated for nearly 16 hours over three days.

Prosecutors said Mr. McDermott went on his rampage because he was angry about the company's plan to comply with an order by the Internal Revenue Service to withhold a large part of his salary to pay back taxes. They said he concocted the Holocaust story after studying how to fake mental illness.

As he was led in shackles from the courtroom, about 50 relatives and friends of the victims stood for sustained applause and yelled, "Die in there!" and "Goodbye!"

Mr. McDermott's parents left without comment.

Prosecutors also cited steps they said Mr. McDermott had taken to plan the killings, including test-firing his shotgun two days earlier and taking the guns to work on Christmas, the day before the killings, when no one was in the office.

—*New York Times*

See, in that article they describe the act. How was I to know, that something bad would happen? I just wish that in my life's history I hadn't developed such a distrust of the Wakefield police department and doing something felt like a worse option than minding my own business.

LAWYERS

Because I am pretty open with broadcasting how I feel about them, I get a lot of lawyer jokes. Someone once told me one that stuck with me:

A lawyer named Jim Fisher was shopping for a tombstone. After he had made his selection, the stonecutter asked him what inscription he would like on it.

"Here lies an honest man and a lawyer," responded the lawyer.

"Sorry, but I can't do that," replied the stonecutter. "In this state, it's against the law to bury two people in the same grave. However, I could put 'Here lies an honest lawyer.'"

"But that won't let people know who it is!" protested the lawyer.

"Sure it will," retorted the stonecutter. "People will read it and exclaim, 'That's impossible!'"

It is a funny story, but I am sad to say that I find the message within it to be painfully and sadly true. I don't know that I blame the legal profession so much as I do the people with whom I'd had negative experiences. After all, my last experience with a lawyer, the woman who took my case for a retainer and told me everything she could find, and then who didn't try to take more money from me, was not a bad one. I guess that I find in my experiences with lawyers frustrations with, more than that group in particular, human nature. People are just greedy. After all, Lorne Buchanan wasn't a lawyer, but that didn't stop him from colluding with people in the legal profession to get his hands on money to which he had no right. Kim wasn't a lawyer, and that didn't stop her from trying every way she could find to screw me over once she decided to give up on our marriage. Greed and anger. I've had enough of those two over my days. Reminds me of that fable by Aesop:

One day a countryman going to the nest of his Goose found there an egg all yellow and glittering. When he took it up it was as heavy as lead and he was going to throw it away, because he thought a trick had been played upon him. But he took it home on second thoughts, and soon found to his delight that it was an egg of pure gold. Every morning the same thing occurred, and he soon became rich by selling his eggs. As he grew rich he grew greedy; and thinking to get at once all the gold the Goose could give, he killed it and opened it only to find nothing.

This fable connects to my story on all sorts of levels. First of all, my father had done everything possible to create a sort of goose that created golden eggs. That is the point of owning rental property, after all. Sure, it takes some work. But if you do those properties right, the income from them never stops coming. Eggs are delivered straight to your bank account once a month in the form of rental checks. Unfortunately, Lorne and Mom wanted more than that monthly form of income. They wanted everything all at once. And once you sell that property, you in essence kill the hen that was supposed to provide for the entire family for years to come.

But I'm also reminded, in that fable of greed, of the way that lawyers operate. It seems that they care very little for sustainable income. After all, there is always another client to dupe. Always another hen to kill. I just grew tired, after all those years, of being on the wrong side of that particular equation. It's my turn to turn the tables.

CONCLUSION

I have now had years to reflect upon the things that have happened to me. I think the reason that I felt so much anger, in addition to my frustrations with feeling dehumanized, were the actions of authorities. I'd say, in retrospect, that their responses to me were a striking combination of mistreatment and apathy. On most occasions, they just didn't do their job. That fostered one particular level of frustration. After all, it was my tax dollars paying their salary. *Your* tax dollars. And they didn't protect me. Who is to say they would protect anyone else? The problem with justice is, it is either applied to everyone or worthless.

Martin Luther King Jr. said it best when he argued that "injustice anywhere is a threat to justice everywhere." What he meant was, we as individuals in a society are either all worthy of respect and rights, or none of us all. Because if the extent of my experiences had been inefficiencies and a lack of professionalism in response to my needs, that would be one thing. But it was much worse. There were other occasions during which police were downright mean.

One occasion when the cops didn't do their jobs, in addition to their failure to prosecute those people who stole our family's money and empire, was when I actually caught—red-handed—Carroll Ayers, my lawyer, forging my own check. The setting of this event was straightforward. I'd been involved in a car accident where I'd been rear-ended while learning to drive an oil truck. I had been interning with an oil truck business when a mattress blew off the top of a car, landed on the windshield of the woman driving a van in front of us, and we rear-ended her. I knew that we were likely to get rear-ended again. Judging by the way we'd stopped, I didn't think people behind us would recognize it quickly enough to stop themselves. We went up to get the kids out.

A state trooper drove up and asked, "Is anyone hurt here?"

"I am. I got thrown into the windshield. I don't know what is up with my back, but it doesn't feel the way it did. There is sort of a pain in my neck."

"OK," the trooper said. "I'll have to report this."

The damage obviously wasn't our fault, and I had a payment coming to me for the treatment of my injuries. I had an idea about what I was owed, especially after the initial interviews with the insurance company.

I expected enough money to cover my medical bills, so I was shocked at the results when Carroll called me into his office. When I arrived, he told me that I was owed seven hundred dollars. When I called to check that number, as I was surprised by how small it was, the insurance company assured me that the check had been written for seven thousand dollars instead. Apparently, Carroll had forgotten a zero in paying me. By this point, I wasn't so surprised with his greed. I'd been down that particular road before with all types of legal professionals. No, I was more shocked with the response of the police. When I went into their offices, with a faxed copy of the check that had been sent to me by the insurance company, the police gave me the runaround.

"I'm here to report a crime," I started out.

They responded to this with the same usual sincerity that I'd come to expect, but I knew it was false. And my fears were confirmed when the police failed to do anything. I mean, the insurance firm had a signed copy of the check for seven thousand dollars, despite the fact that I'd never signed the damn thing. What purer version of forgery could they have hoped for? What could have been a more vivid version of theft? Nonetheless, when I told the police, they did nothing. Did they fear lawyers and so dodge the legal ramifications of my accusations? Did they just not want to do the paperwork? Did they have something against me as a person for some strange and unknown reason? I don't know. But the result was this: now I was out six thousand dollars. I was not then, nor am I now, the kind of rich person who could sustain or easily stomach such a financial loss. But the money meant less to me than the, once again, lowered regard I held for police. I'd always wanted my boys to grow up and be cops. Now, I wondered if something about the job actually erodes a person's ability to do right and care for others.

Another occasion was equally frustrating. During my time driving a tow truck, I'd converted a room in my house into an office. There I paid my bills, kept papers and checks, and kept up with the various things a small business owner has to keep up with. The room I'd chosen as the office was a little sun porch off the back house, the kind of room that is glassed in.

At the time in question, I had a roommate. He'd been a decent tenant for a while, but he had the tendency to, at times, forget to lock the door. Well, one day when I came home from work, I found the door opened. I was frustrated with my roommate, but my feelings escalated to anger when I discovered, upon looking around to see if anything had been taken, that there were some checks missing in my corporate book. These were blank checks— the name said "Ventura Towing and Landscaping"—and I knew that I hadn't just forgotten writing them because they were from the back of my book. I never would have pulled checks from the back of the book, as I had a system and was pretty studious about keeping things organized.

In the face of these missing checks, I began to think the worst about my roommate in a couple of ways. If he hadn't taken the dang things, he was at least at fault. I regret to say that I assumed he'd just stolen them. So I was surprised, and a little embarrassed for that assumption, when I received a call from the bank.

"Mr. Ventura, I have a guy here trying to cash his second check today, and I just wanted to call and check with you,"

"You're kidding," I responded. "It isn't even close to legit. Don't cash it! I'm on my way."

"OK," she said. "Oh gosh, the guy who just tried to cash it is leaving. This is nuts."

"I'll be right there."

It was pretty easy, once we figured out what was going on, to look back at the previous check he'd cashed, which was for five hundred dollars, to see who I'd allegedly made it out to. The name was one I'd never even seen before. But once I started investigating, I found information that cleared my roommate and implicated—you guessed it—a noble officer of the court.

Apparently, a constable had come to deliver papers for me to appear at trial. And when he'd knocked on the door, he'd found it open. So this officer of the court—a paid representative of our arm of justice—helped himself to some of my checks. Pictures of him in the bank cashing the check confirmed that the name on the check, on which he had forged my signature, matched this constable. I did question the intelligence of a person who'd waltz into a bank full of cameras to cash a forged check in the light of day. But I didn't question his smarts so much as I did the ethics of the police, who once again refused to do anything for me. And I questioned the system that—I am not joking here—kept this guy employed and working for the same courts. Nothing ever happened to him.

When someone goes to the beach and picks up sand, if they keep their hand relaxed, the sand will sort of stay where it is. But, when someone exerts a bit of pressure on that sand, it slips more and more quickly through the fingers. My search for justice, my attempt to claim some element of fairness, seemed to just make those things slip more and more quickly from my grasp. Eventually, you get tired of squeezing.

The bank, at least, made sure I got back the money that had been stolen from me. But even then, I had to bring a heavy phrase to get any response. For weeks they dragged their heels on reimbursing my account. But a friend eventually shared with me the magic words, "I'm sorry, Mr. Ventura. We are working on it."

"Well," I'd responded on that day when I finally got some results, "you all keep working on it. And in the meantime, I'm going to call the bank commissioner."

"Excuse me?" she'd said in surprise.

"You heard me. I'll be calling them right after we get off the phone. I'm tired of dealing with this."

"Excuse me, sir. Hold on a minute." After just thirty seconds, she came back on the line. "Mr. Ventura, I'm happy to say that you'll have your money back in no more than two days."

Even in the face of these problems, the thing that stung the most was the outright mistreatment and abuse. I could take inaction a bit more readily than I could outright cruelty. And cruelty is what I eventually got. Cruelty I still don't quite understand. At the time, I was running my tow truck. It was the beginning of a day, so I'd headed over, as was my routine, to the Wakefield Dunkin' Donuts to get my morning coffee. I parked in my uncle's parking which is next to the coffee shop lot. When I went inside everything was as it should be in D & D. The coffee smelled fresh, the doughnuts tempting, and, in the corner, an older woman talked in excited tones about the previous night's Celtics victory. Another normal morning in New England.

But outside, I noticed something abnormal. For one, the door to my truck was open. I'd developed a habit of leaving the truck running, especially during the winter, so that when I got in, it was warm. I was parking in my uncle's parking lot on the side of his rental building, so I didn't worry about the security of the truck. But this morning, as I made my way to the truck that was now off, I began to wonder if I should have developed such a habit.

When I leaned into the truck, I noticed that all papers—registration for the truck, permits for trespass towing, and all the papers from the clipboard with tows that I had done and their corresponding gas receipts—were strewn around the truck as if someone had been looking for something frantically. It was a mess. I'd had everything organized. I saved my receipts because they were tax deductible. And my registration information was as essential to my work as the tow permits. I scratched my head in wonder. *Is this a joke? If it is, I don't find it funny at all!*

As I stood there muttering, the same lady I'd seen in Dunkin' Donuts came over to me. "Excuse me, sir."

"Yes. Did you see what happened here?"

"Yes, I did," she said.

"Well, who did this?"

"Actually, it was police."

"Really?"

"Yeah, I didn't know what they were doing. But they seemed to look a bit mischievous."

This seemed like an odd explanation to me, but I took out my cell phone and dialed the local police station. As the person investigated my questions, I began hearing people laughing in the background. It sounded as if they were in a comedy club, and I didn't understand the humor.

"The guys say that your truck was running, Mr. Ventura."

"OK, is that illegal?"

"Yes, sir, it is."

"Well, I'd sure have preferred a ticket to this. They made a huge mess of all my stuff."

"Well, sir, you shouldn't have left it running."

"Good gosh. What is this conversation? Are you guys a bunch of college-aged practical jokers or the police? And where are my keys?"

I paused as he relayed this question to the officers in the cruiser.

"They say to look around the parking lot."

This is the kind of thing I have faced with the police. And so, when I saw something fishy at that office building, that I thought was a burglary and that instead ended up with seven people dead, is there any wonder that I stayed away from contacting the authorities? Is it any surprise that I just minded my own business? I guess that I would argue, in order to give people more patriotic inclinations and tendencies, it would certainly help if the representatives of the government played their part appropriately.

Ronald Reagan once argued that the scariest words in the English language were "I'm from the government. And I'm here to help." Over the years, as my faith in the government has eroded, I've come to appreciate more and more the sentiments of this wise man.

In conclusion, my theory is that in many instances justice was bought out from under my feet with my own family's money. One case was never heard. Another was unfairly denied to us by legal malpractice. In short, we never got our day in court. Lorne bought off the necessary parties to prevent us from getting our day in court. And Nelson failed to do his job but still got paid for his failure. In neither instance did truth ever really see the light of day.

So why do I keep going? It's simple: my kids. My son Mateo, in particular, has been a blessing to outshine all blessings. Not only do I wake up excited to see him, but I have a newfound motivation to work and to do my best in all areas of life. My desire to be a better father has kept me focused on improving myself in other ways as well. I love my kids so much. And that love perhaps contributed to some of the stress I felt over the years about finances. I don't know if people can ever fully realize the weight of a father's worries when his ability to provide for his family is threatened.

APPENDIX

Page 196—This letter came from the office of Bill Galvin. I wrote in response to an advertisement I saw on TV that asked, "Have you been defrauded?" This was one of the few state agencies that actually helped me. They directed me to the Board of Bar Overseers.

Page 197—Anne Kaufman was my contact person after I received a letter from Bill Galvin's office. She told me that Rosenfeld hadn't worked for the Board of Bar Overseers. She was nonchalant about my case. Furthermore, her office would do nothing about the attorney who had misled me. Yet, her *job* was to look into that sort of thing.

Page 198—This letter was from Doug Nagengast who was perhaps the best—of all the people with whom I spoke—in dodging his professional obligations. No matter what evidence I presented, he refused to do anything about it. All I asked for was an explanation of how what happened *wasn't* criminal.

Page 199, 200—These letters were from the office of the Attorney General, who refused, as well, to investigate the crimes committed against our family. She actually tried to get me arrested for contacting her too frequently. Apparently, calling the Attorney General's Office frequently is not allowed. All I wanted was a referral and some guidance in the right direction.

The Commonwealth of Massachusetts
William Francis Galvin, Secretary of the Commonwealth
Securities Division

January 6, 2010

Mr. Paul Ventura
8 Meadow View Road
Wakefield, MA 01880

Dear Mr. Ventura:

Thank you for contacting the Massachusetts Securities Division (the "Division") regarding your complaint. Based on our phone conversation, and after reviewing all the information, the Division has concluded that the matter falls within the jurisdiction of the Board of Bar Overseers (BBO). Therefore, you should contact the BBO about your complaint:

617-728-8700 Board of Bar Overseers (Boston office)

If you have additional questions, please call the Division and I will be happy to assist you further- I can be reached at 617-727-3548.

Sincerely,

M. Danielle Sherbertes
Enforcement Case Manager

One Ashburton Place, 17th Floor, Boston, Massachusetts 02108 • (617) 727-3548

OFFICE OF THE BAR COUNSEL
BOARD OF BAR OVERSEERS OF THE SUPREME JUDICIAL COURT
99 High Street
Boston. Massachusetts 02110
(617) 728-8750
Fax: (617) 432-2992
www.mass.gov/obcbbo

CONSTANCE V. VECCHIONE
BAR COUNSEL

January 13, 2010

Mr. Paul Ventura
5 Meadow View Road
Wakefield, MA 01880

Dear Mr. Ventura:

We are in receipt of your recent correspondence.

The Office of the Bar Counsel investigates complaints of ethical misconduct against attorneys registered to practice in the Commonwealth of Massachusetts. Our jurisdiction is limited to violations of the Massachusetts Rules of Professional Conduct that regulate the practice of law in this state.

We are unable to identify the attorney with the information given.

Very truly yours,

Anne Kaufman

Anne Kaufman
Assistant Bar Counsel

AK/afln

MIDDLESEX DISTRICT ATTORNEY
15 COMMONWEALTH AVENUE, WOBURN, MA 01801

GERARD T. LEONE JR.
DISTRICT ATTORNEY

Tel: 781-897-6700
Fax: 781-897-6701

April 6, 2010

Paul Ventura
8 Meadow View Road
Wakefield, MA 01880

RE: *Nelson Lovins & Donald Conn*

Dear Mr. Ventura,

I have reviewed the documents that you sent to the Middlesex District Attorney's office that contained allegations of misconduct involving Nelson Lovins and Donald Conn. Based upon our conversations and the documents that you submitted, it appears that any complaint that you may have regarding these individuals would be civil, and not criminal, in nature. Accordingly, the Middlesex District Attorney's Office is not going to investigate this matter further.

Sincerely,

Doug Nagengast
Assistant District Attorney.

APPENDIX

THE COMMONWEALTH OF MASSACHUSETTS
OFFICE OF THE ATTORNEY GENERAL
ONE ASHBURTON PLACE
BOSTON, MASSACHUSETTS 02108-1598

THOMAS F. REILLY
ATTORNEY GENERAL

(617) 727-2200
www.ago.state.ma.us

October 6, 2005

Mr. Paul Ventura
8 Meadow View Road
Wakefield, MA   01880

Dear Mr. Ventura:

The Attorney General's Office has reviewed your recent inquiry to the Criminal Bureau for the purpose of deciding whether to assign this matter within the Criminal Bureau for a more comprehensive review of the facts, make an inquiry on your behalf, or intervene in this matter.

The Criminal Bureau of the Attorney General's Office receives inquiries and complaints on a daily basis from citizens, police departments and other governmental agencies. Every such inquiry and complaint is reviewed and a decision made whether to take action on the inquiry or complaint. In some instances, inquiries and complaints raise issues which generally are not handled by this office, do not fall within this office's jurisdiction, or are more appropriately handled by another agency.

Please be advised that the Criminal Bureau is not going to further review or take action on your inquiry or complaint. If you wish to pursue this matter, I suggest that you contact the appropriate local police department.

I am sorry that this office cannot be of further assistance to you.

Sincerely,

Kurt N. Schwartz
Assistant Attorney General
Chief, Criminal Bureau

KNS/io

THE COMMONWEALTH OF MASSACHUSETTS
OFFICE OF THE ATTORNEY GENERAL
ONE ASHBURTON PLACE
BOSTON, MASSACHUSETTS 02108

MARTHA COAKLEY
ATTORNEY GENERAL

(617) 727-2200
www.mass.gov/ago

November 17, 2010

Paul Ventura
8 Meadow View Road
Wakefield, MA 01880

Dear Mr. Ventura,

The Attorney General's Office has reviewed your recent inquiry or complaint to the Criminal Bureau for the purpose of deciding whether to assign this matter within the Criminal Bureau for a more comprehensive review of the facts, make an inquiry or intervene in this matter.

The Criminal Bureau of the Attorney General's Office receives inquiries and alleged complaints on a daily basis from citizens, police departments and other governmental agencies. Every such inquiry or complaint is reviewed and a decision is made whether to take action on the inquiry or complaint. This type of evaluation is necessary because the volume of complaints and inquiries we receive, coupled with the finite resources available, precludes the Bureau from investigating and prosecuting every allegation that is brought to our attention.

I am advising you that the Criminal Bureau will not be conducting any further review or investigation of your complaint.

I am sorry that this office cannot be of further assistance to you.

Sincerely,

Mary A. Phillips

Mary A. Phillips
Assistant Attorney General
Criminal Bureau

MAP/cb

I would like to offer a final note of criticism to the officials who took an oath to uphold the law, yet refused to investigate one single complaint that I posed over the years. It wasn't that they didn't have knowledge of the problem. I practically shouted from the mountaintops. In meetings requested verbally and dodged, and through the persistent hunt-and-peck typing on my old computer, I tried to raise awareness of many criminal actions to which I'd been victim. I tried to stop those who stole the rewards that had come from Dad's hard work, those reaching greedily for part of his real estate fortune. I wrote close to one hundred letters over the span of several administrations, and not one judge, district attorney, attorney general, or anyone at the Board of Bar Overseers—or any person at any other agency—would do anything to investigate the matters brought forward to them. I know that government officials aren't universally bad. I realize there are exceptions to this pattern of incompetence and outright ignorance. And to all the officials who do stand by the oath of their office, I say this: hats off to you. I commend you and your service. Your actions could have saved what happened to my family and me. I wish that I'd run into a few more government officials that cared like you do. If you have the power, hire more good people! And *please* fire the bad ones. After all—and this is true for everyone, especially public employees—your deeds carry great weight.

Martin Luther King Jr. once wrote that we "are all caught in an inescapable web of mutuality." I agree with King. Our actions can have far-ranging consequences. These events had terrible ramifications not only for my family, but also for my sisters' families and brothers' families. These earthquakes of injustice shook extended family as well. But it did not have to be that way. I think that positive actions can have the same ripple effect across society. All it takes is one person doing the right thing. And others, after witnessing that model behavior, will pay those good deeds forward.

Now I turn to my faith in God to rid me of my sleepless nights. I turn to God, as well, for some semblance of peace in my endless days of investigating how and why people betrayed my family. I've heard that I should "let go and let God," which I interpret as offering up to God those things in my life that are too big to deal with or change. And now it seems I've done all I can. So I now offer up to God this story and the responsibility to help me understand everything that has happened. I can go no farther on this journey—now thirty years long—for justice. I have done all I can to show people that what they did and how they responded to my pleas for help was wrong.

I'd like to make one final point. I am aware of people's opinions regarding my pursuit of justice. Understandably, they haven't shared my burning desire to right these wrongs. I've often been viewed as a raving lunatic. And people will think what they think. I know I have issues. (Doesn't everyone?) I know that struggling to sleep, having the same thing circle through my brain again and again without any chance of reprieve or solution, is not normal. But the circumstances that made me that sort of person were forced upon me. We can't choose the hand we've been dealt. I've heard people say you choose the way you play the hand. But what about the people whose hand is rigged? What if, even when we play our hand the best we can, we still lose? What happens when those in charge, those who make or enforce the rules, don't do their job? When I learned just how unfair the world could be, I couldn't sit idly by. I hope, after reading this book, people will understand that my erratic behavior—on many occasions—was somewhat justified by what I've been put through. In other words, I'm not crazy—just insane with anger.

Now I end my fight for justice for the Ventura family. But I'd like to leave you, my readers, to ponder a few final questions: How could this happen? Was this justice for the Ventura family? What does this say about our justice system in general? How would you feel—to apply the Golden Rule in this particular instance—if this had happened to you? Is the difference in this country between "moral" and "legal" something with which you are comfortable? Consider this my final plea, my final attempt to bring justice to the Ventura family.